New Mags City Guide
Berlin

For years, I've traveled the world as a design and lifestyle expert. Every time I discover an inspiring place, I make a note of it. Over time, this list has grown to include many outstanding destinations. People often ask me for travel recommendations. Obviously, most people don't have the time to find the best spots, because it requires time, and time is a scarce resource for many. That's why we created this series of city guides. Not just any collection of guides, but the best, most beautiful, and most practical, presented as a real book. I believe the ideal city guide is tangible, something you can bring along on your journey, especially handy when your smartphone runs out of battery.

Special thanks to Jesper Svangård from New Mags for his enthusiasm and publishing expertise, and to Mario Depicolzuane, our art director, whose studio's design brought this guide to life. I'm also deeply grateful to all the incredible locations featured and to everyone who helped bring this project to life.

We hope that you, as a reader, will embrace our city guide and find it valuable on your travels. After all, that's the true purpose of this book.

ROSA-LUXEMBURG-PLATZ

Allianz

Berlin is a city of contrasts, constantly reinventing itself through art, music, and history.

After the fall of the Wall in 1989, it became a creative playground: abandoned apartments, warehouses, and factories turned into studios, clubs, and galleries. This raw freedom also gave birth to the underground music scene where techno culture and other genres were born. Quite literally underground, many raves took place in abandoned concrete bunkers below the city.

Berlin's urban identity, particularly in the former East, offered cheap studios and housing that transformed the city into one of Europe's cultural hubs. Artists, musicians, and designers poured in from around the world, attracted by the combination of affordability, space, and an international outlook that encouraged collaboration across borders and disciplines.

By the early 2000s, Berlin was crowned Europe's "upcoming city." Magazines like Wallpaper* and Monocle declared it the continent's creative capital, and in 2003 Mayor Klaus Wowereit famously branded it "poor but sexy." Galleries bloomed in Mitte, while Kreuzberg and Neukölln became synonymous with a new European bohemia. And yet Berlin's paradox remains: the city has always been declared "finished," yet never stops becoming. Once raw, cheap, and punk, it is now more polished and curated. Where Berliners once queued all night for Berghain, they now line up for morning croissants and flat whites. But its DNA, freedom, creativity, and nightlife, still keeps it forever on the verge of reinvention.

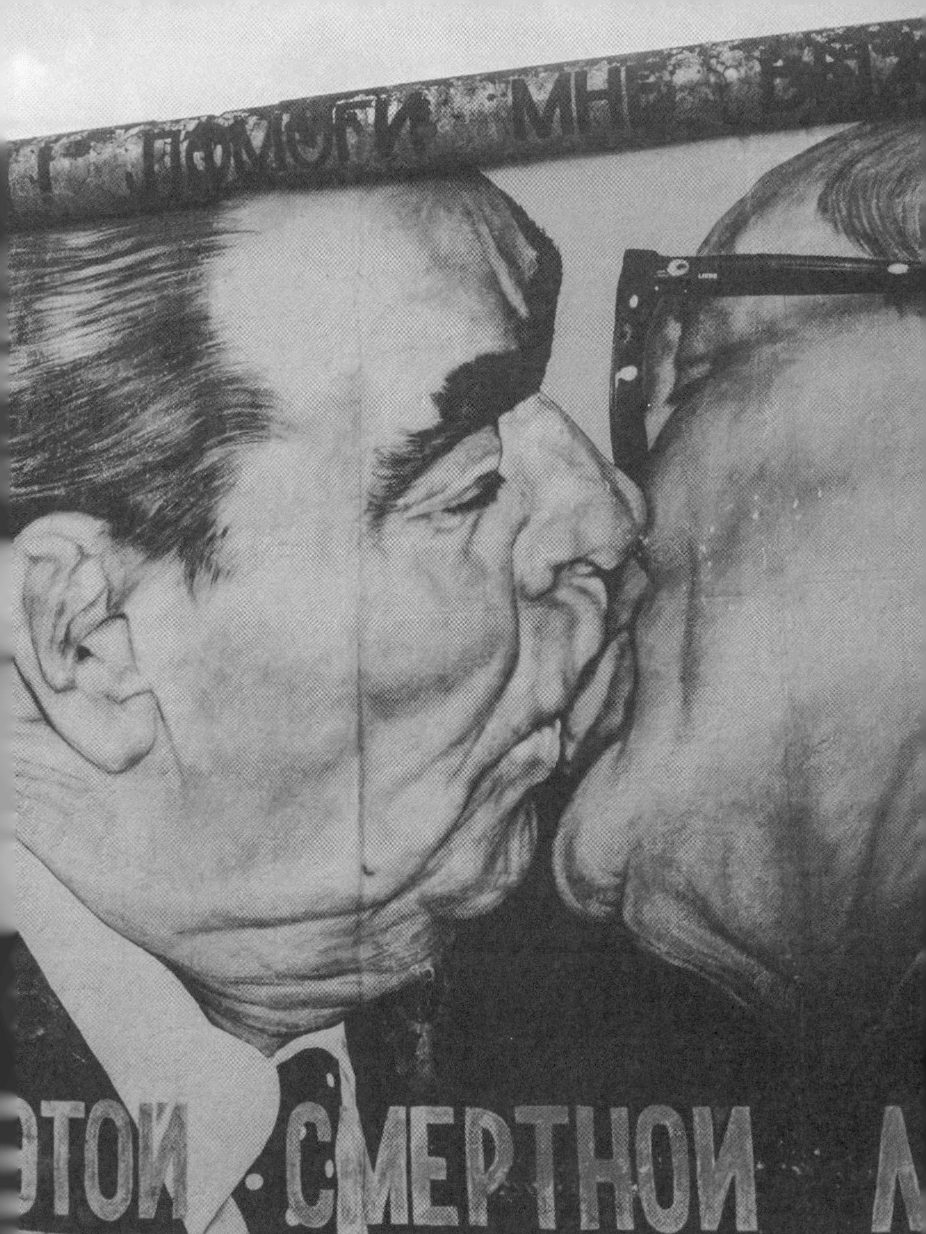
ПОМОГИ МНЕ
ЭТОИ СМЕРТНОИ

Hotel Telegraphenamt
MM:NT
25hours Hotel Bikini Berlin
SO/Berlin Das Stue
Gorki Apartments
The Circus Hotel
Michelberger Hotel
Locke At Eastside Gallery
The Hoxton Charlottenburg
Wilmina

Stay

Hotel Telegraphenamt

Monbijoustrasse 11
10117 Berlin

@telegraphenamt.berlin
telegraphenamt.com
+49 309940590

Messages once flew out from here to every corner of the world. Built in 1910 as Berlin's main telegraph office, this neo-baroque landmark was once the city's communications hub. Today it's Telegraphenamt, a boutique hotel where history and design collide in spectacular fashion.

The restoration has left the drama intact; vaulted ceilings, mosaic floors, exposed brick, layered with sleek interiors by Dreimeta. Step into the lobby and you'll spot the original pneumatic tube system, a wink to its past life. Upstairs, 97 rooms and maisonettes balance raw character with modern comfort. Floor-to-ceiling windows open to cinematic views: Monbijoupark, Berlin Cathedral, the TV Tower.

Root, the orangery-style restaurant, is filled with hanging plants, lanterns, and bold flavours, from sushi to grilled classics. The bar, lined with plush red stools, is a late-night destination in itself. Breakfast in the former workrooms adds one more story to the building's long history of communication.

With its mix of heritage, design, and location, steps from Fotografiska, Hackesche Höfe, and Museum Island, Telegraphenamt is a Berlin landmark reimagined, a place that still connects people.

Back in the days, this building sent up to 20,000 telegrams a day. Today, it's more likely text messages flying out from Telegraphenamt.

00 01

MM:NT

An d. Spandauer Brücke 11
10178 Berlin

@mmnt_intime
mmnt-intime.com
+49 15226025318

The world's first 'beta hotel' MM:NT Berlin Lab opened in Mitte in 2024. It isn't finished, but that's the whole idea. This is Berlin, after all: six rooms, modular communal spaces, and a digital-first set-up where your phone runs the show. Guests shape the concept in real time, leaving feedback that literally changes the future of hospitality.

Rooms come in three sizes, Little, Middle, Big, but keep the same stripped-back aesthetic: warm minimalism, clever storage, and everything you actually need (extra pillows, robes, hair straighteners, even toasters) available on demand. The idea? Less clutter, more flexibility, and a stay you can hack to your own rhythm.

Communal areas double as playgrounds for connection. The Lounge mixes co-working vibes with beer and wine taps you activate via app. The Box system holds all the extras, ready when you need them, keeping rooms uncluttered and the vibe simple.

Conscious design runs through it all: reused and recycled materials, green energy powering the app, and a manifesto for low-impact stays. MM:NT is scrappy, agile, always in motion. Less polished, more prototype. Very Berlin.

Why stay in a finished hotel, when you can be part of one still in the making.

25hours Hotel Bikini Berlin

Budapester Strasse 40
10787 Berlin

@25hourshotelbikiniberlin
25hours-hotels.com
+49 301202210

Founded in Hamburg, 25hours Hotels stands for playful design, social spaces, and a touch of irreverence. The Berlin outpost, opened in 2014, was their first in the city, and they chose a landmark: the legendary 1950s Bikinihaus. The hotel bridges past and present: on one side the bustle of Breitscheidplatz and the Kaiser Wilhelm Memorial Church, on the other the leafy canopy of Berlin Zoo, monkeys and all.

The 149 rooms are split between Urban and Jungle categories, with exposed concrete, floor-to-ceiling windows, and quirky extras like hammocks, Schindelhauer bikes, or freestanding bathtubs in the larger suites. Rooms are colourful, informal, and fun, exactly the spirit of 25hours.

Public spaces amplify the vibe: Monkey Bar has become one of the city's favourite rooftop spots, buzzing with DJs, cocktails, and a wraparound terrace, while NENI serves vibrant Middle Eastern–Mediterranean food beneath a greenhouse-style canopy of plants. Downstairs, the Aperitivo Bar keeps the energy going with coffee, pastries, and snacks throughout the day.

Dubbed “Bikinihaus” in the 1950s for its bare midriff design, the name stuck. When 25hours opened here in 2014, they kept the name.

SO/Berlin Das Stue

Drakestrasse 1
10787 Berlin

@soberlin.das.stue
so-berlin-das-stue.com
+49 303117220

Housed in a former 1930s embassy building, SO/Berlin Das Stue still feels like the grand living room of Berlin's diplomatic quarter, only with better cocktails. With 78 rooms and suites, it's intimate yet opulent, where clean-lined interiors by Patricia Urquiola meet sweeping views over the Tiergarten and Berlin Zoo. Some suites even give you eye contact with ostriches and antelopes. Inside, the mood is elegant but playful. The lobby doubles as an art-filled salon, the libraries host intimate events, and the Stue Bar mixes high-end drinks in a setting that feels equal parts design studio and private club. In summer, the terrace is a leafy oasis, complete with its own discreet entrance straight into the zoo.

Dining is French with a Berlin twist. Carte Blanche serves brasserie classics, perfectly grilled entrecôte, truffle pasta, crème Brûlée, executed in a warm, unfussy room. Downstairs, the Susanne Kaufmann spa stretches across 260 m^2, with a pool, sauna, and treatments designed for full reset mode.

Das Stue means 'living room', and that's the vibe. Elegant, intimate, and with the Berlin Zoo literally in your backyard.

Gorki Apartments

Weinbergsweg 25
10119 Berlin

@gorkiapartments
gorkiapartments.com
+49 3048496480

Checking into Gorki feels less like a hotel stay and more like inheriting the keys to a very chic Berlin neighbour's flat. Hidden behind a leafy courtyard in Mitte, this Wilhelminian-era house has been reimagined into 34 apartments and two penthouses, each with its own quirks, mailboxes, doorbells, even names on the doors instead of numbers. Lea Grün, Herr Günther... you'll feel like you've moved in rather than checked in.

Inside, the vibe is classic Berlin: raw plaster walls, high stucco ceilings, and a curated mix of design classics and flea-market treasures. Every apartment has its own personality, some elegant, some eclectic, all very stylish. Kitchens and generous floorplans make it easy to live like a local, while the round-the-clock reception team adds a boutique-hotel level of service. And yes, dogs are as welcome as humans.

Gorki nails that Berlin paradox of rough edges and refined taste. It's a place for longer stays, creative escapes, or simply pretending you've relocated to Mitte. Step outside and you're surrounded by cool cafés, wine bars, trendy galleries, and buzzy nightlife. Step back in and it's your own private sanctuary, a home, a hideout, and a slice of Berlin cool.

At Gorki, doors have names instead of numbers, Lea Grün, Herr Günther, so it feels like you're moving into a neighbour's flat, not checking into a hotel.

The Circus Hotel

Rosenthaler Strasse 1
10119 Berlin

@thecircus_berlin
circus-berlin.de
+49 3020003939

Rosenthaler Platz is Berlin in microcosm, creative, chaotic, and impossible to pin down. Right in the middle of it all sits The Circus Hotel, a boutique hotel that's been part of Mitte's cultural fabric since the early 2000s. Inside, the vibe is design-forward but playful. Designer Sandra Ernst gave each room its own identity, while the hotel's shared spaces double as mini galleries, showing works by artists like Elisa Stozyk and Stefanie Hering. There's a cosy courtyard, a rooftop terrace with an honesty bar, and plenty of corners to linger with a drink or a book.

But what makes the Circus Hotel stand out is its Behind the Curtain programme, curated tours and activities exclusive to guests. Forget the clichés; this is where you dive into queer history, neighbourhood street food, Berlin's wild architecture, and underground art scenes. It's like having the keys to the city handed to you, minus the tourist traps. It's Berlin, uncovered.

The Circus Hotel isn't just a hotel, it's your backstage pass to Berlin's true face.

Michelberger Hotel

Warschauer Strasse 39–40
10243 Berlin

@michelbergerhotel
michelbergerhotel.com
+49 3029778590

Since 2009, Michelberger has helped shape Friedrichshain into one of Berlin's coolest neighbourhoods. Housed in a former factory on the border to Kreuzberg, the hotel has always been more than a place to stay, it's a communal house where art, design, and hospitality blur together. Nadine and Tom Michelberger set the tone from the beginning, and today international travellers and locals still mingle here over coffee, concerts, or late-night cocktails.

The transformation of the building has been guided by architects Werner Aisslinger and Sigurd Larsen, and designer Jonathan Tuckey, giving the interiors a playful yet comforting edge. Above it all, 140 rooms cater to every budget, from smaller "cosy" rooms to loft-like suites, while downstairs is a world of shared spaces.

The breakfast alone is worth checking in for: organic products from local producers, served in an atmosphere that makes you want to linger. Or simply start with the lobby café's locally roasted coffee, organic lunches, and homemade pastries before the space shifts into evenings of natural wine, handcrafted cocktails, and conversation. The lush courtyard and in-house restaurant add another layer, grounding the urban energy in something slower and more organic.

Since 2009, Michelberger has defined what a community-driven design hotel can be in Berlin.

Locke At Eastside Gallery

Mühlenstrasse 61–63
10243 Berlin

@lockehotels
lockeliving.com
+49 307262 98540

Locke does hotels differently. Think studios with kitchens, co-working spaces, and bars designed to bring people together. Their first Berlin outpost opened in 2023, right on the Spree, with front-row views of the East Side Gallery. On one side: Friedrichshain. On the other: Kreuzberg. Mitte just up the road.

There are 176 apartments here, each with a lived-in vibe, raw concrete softened with warm timber, braided rugs, turmeric chairs, pastel mirrors. Some come with balconies over the river, others with skyline views. All feel like places you could actually stay a while, not just crash for the night.

At the ground floor, ANIMA, the hotel's listening bar and restaurant, riffs on Japan's hi-fi Kissaten cafés. By day it's coffee from Bonanza and natural wines by Ritual; by night it's vinyl, DJs, and Mediterranean-leaning small plates. The kind of spot where you order another round just to hear one more track.

There's also a gym with floor-to-ceiling windows, a rooftop for events, and plenty of co-working space if you really must open your laptop. But the point of Locke is clear: part hotel, part hangout, part slice of Berlin life.

Locke at Eastside Gallery in Friedrichshain, Berlin's grit, Kreuzberg's cool, and the Spree right outside your window.

NEUE WELT

The Hoxton Charlottenburg

Meinekestrasse 18–19
10719 Berlin

@thehoxtonhotel
thehoxton.com
+49 30233218460

The Hoxton's German debut had to make a statement, and where better than Charlottenburg. Just off Ku'damm, the city's iconic shopping avenue, The Hox landed in 2023 with 234 rooms and its signature open-house spirit.

Inside, the look is "rough nouveau", a mash-up of Charlottenburg's golden-era glamour and Berlin's brutalist edge. Expect unrefined plaster walls paired with Art Deco lighting, vintage finds set against emerald tiles, and a lobby dominated by a bespoke mural from local artist Stefanie Kägi. Public spaces are layered and textured, Murano chandeliers over Bauhaus furniture, a wraparound bar leading to a Winter Garden, and plenty of corners to linger with coffee or cocktails.

Food and drink are equally bold. House of Tandoor serves up spice-driven Indian sharing plates cooked in copper tandoor ovens, while The Teahouse takes you from masala chai in the morning to cocktails by night. Add in The Apartment, a 1920s-style events space under the eaves, and you've got one of West Berlin's hottest new hangouts.

As with every Hoxton, the hotel doubles as a community hub. Local collabs with Record Magazine and Berlin makers stock the Hox Shop and soundtrack the lobby turntables.

Check into The Hoxton and step straight into West Berlin's golden-era chic, recast for today.

Wilmina

Kantstrasse 79
10627 Berlin

@wilmina
wilmina.com
+49 302018050

Tucked away in Charlottenburg, Wilmina is unlike any other Berlin stay. Once a courthouse and women's prison, the ensemble has been radically transformed by Grüntuch Ernst Architects into a serene hideout of gardens, courtyards, and quiet luxury. Behind its austere walls you now find 44 individually designed rooms, a rooftop terrace, spa, pool, and library, all wrapped in soft light and soothing textures. Think monastic calm meets contemporary design.

The heart of the house is Lovis, Sophia Rudolph's contemporary German restaurant, hidden in the old prison yard and now framed by panoramic windows onto lush greenery. Listed in the Michelin Guide and among the World's 50 Best Discovery Restaurants, it's where fine dining feels grounded and modern at once. Next door, the Lovis Bar plays with flavours rather than labels, while Lotta Tagesbar and Wilmina Brot connect the project to the neighbourhood with aperitivos, fresh bakes, and sourdough rooted in Berlin tradition.

What could have stayed a heavy monument to the past is now reimagined as a sanctuary, part retreat, part cultural space, with the adjacent Amtsalon hosting art, design, and architecture projects. Hidden, yet right in the middle of Charlottenburg, Wilmina is one of Berlin's most poetic reinventions.

From cells to suites. Wilmina is one of Berlin's most poetic transformations.

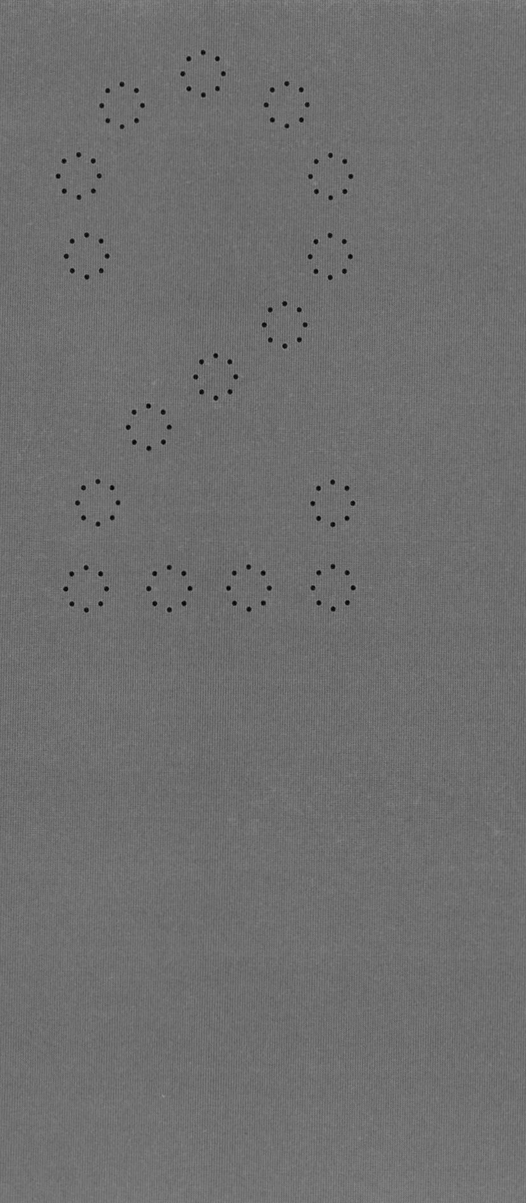

Acid Café
Annelies
Coffee Circle Café
Zeit für Brot
Frea Bakery
Keit
Café Einstein Unter den Linden
Bonanza Coffee Roasters
Chipperfield Kantine
Chungking Noodles
Clärchens Ballhaus
Aerde
Father Carpenter
Borchardt
Remi
Frieda
JaJa
ORA Restaurant & Wine Bar
Il Ritrovo
Freundschaft
Paris Bar
Green Door
Prater Biergarten

Taste

Donald Judd Writings

Acid Café

Christinenstrasse 19a
10119 Berlin

@acid.cafe

A Madrid original reimagined for Berlin, Acid Café brings its quietly radical coffee philosophy to a concrete corner of Prenzlauer Berg, facing Teutoburger Platz. Designed by Studio Plantea in collaboration with Danish design brand Frama, the space reflects a dialogue between architecture and atmosphere, minimalistic, yet deeply sensory.

Once a cool, geometric shell of concrete and steel, the interior was softened through crafted interventions: a warm chestnut wood structure enclosing the staircase, sculptural speakers that define the soundscape, and a stainless-steel counter where coffee and conversation unfold in harmony. Along the facade, Frama chairs with woven seats, delicate Wendy Taylor lamps, and a curated display of objects and ceramics introduce warmth and tactility.

More than a café, Acid feels like a spatial composition. It's a place that turns precision into poetry, where design, music, and caffeine meet under one serene, amber-lit glow.

Born in Madrid, Acid Café's Berlin space fuses
Southern warmth with the city's signature roughness.

Annelies

Görlitzer Strasse 68
10997 Berlin

@anneliesberlin

Come morning, Annelies pulls a cool crowd like no other. Stylish content creators, foodie hunters, young Koreans and Japanese fashionistas, even locals with strollers and kids line up in front of Görlitzer Park. By Saturday noon, the line is a Berlin ritual in itself.

Is Berlin's most-hyped breakfast spot really worth the wait? Absolutely.

The reason is simple: annelies is far from your average breakfast joint. A short menu of just eight dishes, each one crafted with the kind of precision you'd expect at dinner, not with your morning coffee.

Three are non-negotiables: the sesame pancake bun stuffed with sausage, egg and cheese; scrambled eggs on sourdough topped with grated smoked yolk; and the pillowy buttermilk pancakes, layered and indulgent. Seasonal specials rotate in, but the staples are already legendary.

The vibe is unfussy and effortlessly insta-cool, and the grungy backdrop of Görlitzer Park sets the perfect Kreuzberg vibe. There are no reservations, so set an alarm and be ready to wait in line. Do your 5k run beforehand, you won't want to skip dessert here.

Coffee Circle Café

Lindower Strasse 18
13347 Berlin

@coffeecircle
coffeecircle.com

Coffee Circle's flagship café sits in a historic 1905 brick building in Wedding, right next to their roastery. Since 2016, the fragrance of freshly roasted beans has drifted through the neighborhood, quietly reshaping the area around Nettelbeckplatz. Inside, the café is all muted tones and clean design, a calm counterpoint to the graffiti-streaked housing blocks and neon kiosks just outside.

Founded in 2010 as an online coffee brand with a focus on social projects, Coffee Circle's move into this physical space gave the company a new identity. Today, it feels like both a café and a statement: transparent sourcing, fair trade, and a dedication that won them the Specialty Coffee Association's Sustainability Award in 2022.

On the menu, two espressos and two filters are always in rotation, ranging from classic chocolatey roasts to fruity, experimental single origins. Guests sip their brews under high window arches, tucked into the mezzanine, or out front on the quiet cul-de-sac. It's not just a café, but a sign of Wedding's changing energy, young creatives and locals alike anchoring their day with a shot of Cerrado or a pour-over from Ethiopian Limu.

Zeit für Brot

Alte Schönhauser Strasse 4
10119 Berlin

@zeitfuerbrot
zeitfuerbrot.com
+49 30 28046780

Since 2012, the smell of freshly baked bread has drifted down Alte Schönhauser Straße, where Zeit für Brot opened its first Berlin bakery. Founded in Frankfurt in 2009, the concept was simple: honour craftsmanship, use only organic ingredients, and bake everything on-site with long fermentation and no additives.

The Mitte bakery feels like a stage set for bread lovers. Behind glass walls, bakers fold, shape, and glaze, while queues stretch down the street, especially on weekends. Locals, travellers, and a strong gen-Z crowd line up for the signature Zimtschnecken (cinnamon buns), which have become as much an Instagram ritual as a breakfast treat. The sourdough loaves are excellent, but the sticky spirals, warm from the oven, are the real cult item.

From this first branch, Zeit für Brot has expanded across Berlin (Prenzlauer Berg, Charlottenburg, Wilmersdorf) and into other German cities. In 2025, it opened in London's Islington, exporting Berlin's bread fairy tale to a new generation of fans.

Always busy, always worth the wait. Zeit für Brot turns long queues into Berlin's sweetest ritual.

Frea Bakery

Gartenstraße 9
10115 Berlin

@freabakery
freabakery.de
+493013897068

Tucked into a quieter corner of Mitte, Frea Bakery is the bakery-cousin to the famed FREA restaurant, and shares its ethos of "full taste, zero waste." Since its 2022 opening, the founders have insisted on plant-based, regional, seasonal ingredients and a closed-loop waste system.

The pastries are fully vegan, with signatures like a cardamom croissant, spandauer cups, and croissants made using a house-developed margarine instead of butter. Every crumb counts: leftover baguettes become croutons, breadcrumbs ferment into bread miso, and unsold pastries are composted on site. Their "Gersi" compost machine transforms kitchen scraps into soil in 24 hours, feeding back to the farms.

Inside, the bakery is warm and welcoming, wood, soft lighting, natural tones , complemented by a summer terrace. Guests can drop by for fresh sourdough loaves, seasonal lunches, juices, or a quiet coffee moment. With its seamless blend of sustainability, design, and flavor, Frea Bakery feels like a quietly radical portrait of what Berlin's modern bakery can be.

Keit

Graefestrasse 7
10967 Berlin

@keit.berlin
keit.berlin

Keit began in 2019, when former adidas colleagues Thanos Petalotis and Kolja Orzeszko traded sneakers for sourdough. Their vision was clear: bake bread with integrity, using organic grains sourced within 100 km of Berlin, and keep the process rooted in sustainability, reliability, and gratitude.

The first bakery opened in Schöneberg, offering little more than a single sourdough loaf. Word spread quickly, and the range expanded to rye, spelt, baguettes, and rolls. Soon after came a second location on Grünberger Straße in Friedrichshain, cementing Keit as one of the city's most exciting new bakeries.

In 2025, Keit unveiled its third and most ambitious space: a Kreuzberg flagship designed by Studio Michael Burman. Here, an old millstone anchors the counter, handmade washi paper wraps the walls, and Douglas fir benches invite quiet pause.

EINSTEIN

Café Einstein Unter den Linden

Unter den Linden 42
10117 Berlin

@einsteinunterdenlinden
einstein-udl.com
+49 302043632

Albert Einstein spent defining years in Berlin, making it only fitting that cafés here still carry his name as a nod to both intellect and old-world elegance. Café Einstein Unter den Linden is one of those places that feels timeless in a city that changes by the minute.

Opened in 1996 by Gerald Uhlig in a historic villa once owned by German movie star Henny Porten, it captures the spirit of 1920s Berlin mixed with Viennese coffeehouse charm. Politicians and journalists come for its discretion and its location close to the government quarter and media houses, while locals and tourists alike are drawn to the sense of tradition, or simply to the fizzy drinks and what many call the best Wiener Schnitzel in town.

The interior matches the mood: parquet floors, marble-topped tables, dark wood booths, and old photographs on the walls, with waiters in crisp uniforms gliding effortlessly between tables. The menu focuses on seasonal and often organic ingredients, with classics that are hard to resist, schnitzel, goulash, and apple strudel prepared just as they should be.

Bonanza Coffee Roasters

Adalbertstrasse 70
10999 Berlin

@bonanzacoffee
bonanzacoffee.de

This isn't just a roastery with a token espresso machine, it's a place built around the craft of coffee, from bean to cup. Since 2006, the Kreuzberg roastery has, in their own words, been pushing "too far" in pursuit of flavour clarity. No dark roasts, no shortcuts, just beans treated with obsessive care and brewed to let terroir, not technique, do the talking.

Bonanza is really for coffee believers. It's not the place for extra-shot lattes or laptop marathons, but for pausing, tasting, and paying attention. Forget labels like hipster or bougie; Bonanza takes roasting and extraction seriously, and the results speak for themselves.

The flagship café, hidden in a quiet courtyard off Adalbertstraße, feels like a modernist greenhouse: industrial style interior in glass, steel, and soft wood, flooded in warm sunlight.

The pastries are worth the detour too. Try the oversized, golden apple turnovers and almond croissants that pair beautifully with a filter or flat white. For coffee enthusiasts, adventurers, and anyone curious about flavour at its purest, Bonanza is a must.

Chipperfield Kantine

Joachimstrasse 11
10119 Berlin

@chipperfieldkantine
chipperfield-kantine.de
+49 30280170781

Situated in the heart of Berlin, near Rosenthaler Platz, the Chipperfield Kantine is part of an office campus created by David Chipperfield Architects. This campus combines four modern office buildings with a former piano factory from 1895.

The design of the Kantine‘s cubic building is characterised by interiors featuring exposed concrete, wood, and marble. The building itself, the furniture, tableware, and cutlery was thoughtfully designed by David Chipperfield and his team. The Kantine is open not just to staff but also to the public. During the summer, the garden beneath the plane trees becomes a popular meeting place for both locals and visitors. It’s an ideal spot for lunch, informal meetings, or just a coffee. The open kitchen allows guests to feel part of the community, watching the chefs at work.

Chungking Noodles

Reichenberger Strasse 35
10999 Berlin

@chungkingnoodles

What started as a supper club and a series of pop-ups has become one of Berlin's most cult dining rooms. Shanghai-born chef Ash Lee first introduced Berliners to the fiery flavours of Chongqing back in 2017, before opening her Kreuzberg spot in 2019. The focus is singular and obsessive: Chongqing xiao mian, the iconic noodle dish from southwestern China, served here with unapologetic heat and numbing Sichuan pepper.

The menu is short and sharp. Handmade wheat noodles come drenched in Ash's house-made chili oil, numbing with Sichuan pepper and layered with spice. Variations include minced pork, braised beef, or a vegan tofu-shiitake version, with the odd special like chicken gizzards. Sides run from pickled cucumber to Sichuan sausage (made in Berlin by The Sausage Man Never Sleeps), and a custom Chungking Pale Ale.

Martino Sacci from Rhizomet Architects designed the interior, with the open kitchen and its bright red tiled bar as the central feature. Behind it, a simply furnished dining room opens up, combining industrial touches with playful colours. Grey walls meet cream tiles with pink grout, while light wood tables, stools, and benches line the space, giving it warmth against the raw urban backdrop of Reichenberger Strasse.

The vibrant streets of Sichuan come alive at Berlin's hippest noodle cult, Chungking Noodles.

Clärchens Ballhaus

Auguststrasse 24/25
10117 Berlin

@claerchens_ballhaus
claerchensball.haus
+49 30400698100

Few places capture Berlin's soul quite like Clärchens Ballhaus. Opened in 1913 by Fritz Bühler and his wife Clara, it has carried the city through two world wars, six currency reforms, and reunification, scarred in places, but never losing its charm. Just before the end of the Second World War, a bomb destroyed the front building, and "Clärchen" Clara Habermann herself moved into a small flat next to the Spiegelsaal, where she lived until her death in 1971. Today, the glamorous 350 m²
Hall of Mirrors and rustic restaurant host old-school dancing and Berlin classics. Expect Königsberger Klopse or Wackelpudding, house wine straight from the barrel, and on Sundays, the legendary Schwoof: swing, salsa, tango, and foxtrot until late evening.

Clärchens Ballhaus is one of the most extraordinary places in Berlin, a house where the spirit of pre-war Berlin still lingers in the creaking floors, the faded mirrors, and the air itself. No place is quite like it.

Aerde

Am Lokdepot 6
10965 Berlin

@aerde.berlin
aerde.de

What first catches the eye at Aerde is its home: a striking red-brick building at the edge of Park Gleisdreieck, part of the Lokdepot complex by Robertneun.

Here on the border of Schöneberg and Kreuzberg, aerde feels less like a restaurant and more like a research lab for flavour. Founded by Justus Will and led together with Hillevi Hövelmann, and head chef Igor Kazakov in the kitchen, it's a project deeply rooted in the forests and fields around Berlin.

The philosophy is bold but simple: to take the raw, natural essence of local ingredients and elevate them with a modern, precise twist. The result is a menu that leans vegetarian, with the option of fish or meat courses, always guided by what's fresh and seasonal.

The dining room holds just 20 seats, with interiors by Keenan Rush and Anselmo Custer giving the space a Nordic-inspired, pared-back feel. The eight-seat Chef's Table anchors the room, framed by Enea Toldo's clay installation, while natural wines and thoughtful non-alcoholic pairings complete the experience.

Behind the scenes, the team also works from a lakeside research space in Wendisch-Rietz, where they experiment with ingredients from the forest. Studies that might end up as a dish on your plate in Berlin.

Aerde turns the forests and fields around Berlin into fine dining with a quiet, radical edge.

F
C
TABLE SERVICE
F
C
CAFE
FATHER
CARPENTER

Father Carpenter

Münzstrasse 21
10178 Berlin

@father.carpenter
fathercarpenter.com

Step off Münzstraße and into a vaulted courtyard, and you'll stumble upon Father Carpenter, a leafy hideaway that feels miles away from the bustle of Mitte. Whitewashed walls, warm wood, and sunlit tables set a calm, unhurried tone.

Founded in 2015 by Melbourne-raised Kresten Thøgersen, the café grew from a modest pop-up into one of Berlin's most beloved coffee and brunch institutions. Rooted in Australia's café culture, it quickly developed a reputation for precision brewing and thoughtful hospitality. Along the way, Thøgersen co-founded Fjord Coffee Roasters with Silo Coffee before launching Father Carpenter's own independent roastery in 2023, dedicated to light roasts that highlight terroir and clarity of flavour.

The food is as carefully balanced as the coffee: pulled-pork Benedicts, avocado toast with feta and chili, millet porridge, and vegan banana bread have become modern classics.

In summer 2025, the brand expanded with a minimalist coffee bar in Schönleinstrasse, Kreuzberg, focusing only on serving their lightly roasted coffees.

borchardt RESTAURANT

Borchardt

Französische Strasse 47
10117 Berlin

@restaurant_borchardt
borchardt-restaurant.de
+49 3081886262

Few restaurants in Berlin carry as much myth and momentum as Borchardt. Established in 1853, surving two world wars, and revived after reunification, it has long been a stage for the Berlin crowd. The Kaiser once dined here, and in more recent decades Karl Lagerfeld, Angela Merkel, Johnny Depp, and George Clooney have followed—just to name a few. Today it remains the power-lunch address of choice for politicians, media executives, fashion insiders and visiting celebrities, especially during Fashion Week, when the terrace becomes a catwalk of its own. As in Paris, there's a special allure when old-school institutions suddenly feel like the hottest place in town.

Inside, the look is classic Berlin grandeur: high stucco ceilings, columns, dark red banquettes and a dining room buzzing with quiet drama. The service is polished, the atmosphere equal parts elegant and theatrical. Guests may claim they come for the food, but they also come to be seen. Still, the kitchen holds its own. The Wiener Schnitzel, golden and paper-thin, is a citywide legend, and staples like oysters, veal entrecôte and Béarnaise sauce anchor a menu that blends German and French tradition.

With nearly two hundred years of excellence in the Berlin food scene, Borchardt offers a historic dining experience.

Remi

Torstrasse 48
10119 Berlin

@restaurant_remi
remi-berlin.de
+49 3027593090

Located on the ground floor of the architecturally striking Suhrkamp Verlag building in Berlin-Mitte, Remi is a contemporary brasserie inspired by Dutch and French culinary traditions. Designed by renowned architect Roger Bundschuh, the building captivates with its clean lines, high ceilings, glass façades, and raw concrete, creating a bold, urban atmosphere that stands out in Berlin. The interior has been thoughtfully crafted by Berlin-based designer Ester Bruzkus, bringing warmth and sophistication to the space.

The kitchen at Remi follows a refined, minimalist approach, focusing on the essence of each ingredient. Dishes are inspired by Dutch and French cuisine and prepared with fresh, seasonal products sourced primarily from the Berlin region. The result is elegant, understated cuisine that lets the quality of the ingredients shine, without unnecessary embellishments.

Remi is located inside Olafur Eliasson's striking glass atrium on Torstraße.

Neighbourhoods

Berlin

KAUFHAU

ESTENS
VOGUE

A cityscape is defined by the sum of its neighbourhoods. They are the heartbeat of a city, infusing life and diversity into its very soul. Some are artsy and vibrant, others are more serene and exclusive. Each neighbourhood has its own unique character, and we all have our favourite areas that we feel connected to. In this section, we break down the city and introduce you to the coolest neighbourhoods. All the locations in the book, along with a few bonus spots, are marked on detailed neighbourhood maps, making it easy for you to discover your favourite district.

Fight fascism -
smash capitalism
ife
is
¡A
RISK!

bleibt!

9
4
7
3
8
2
5
1
6

Charlottenburg-Wilmersdorf

			Don't Miss:
1	The Hoxton Charlottenburg (p. 49)	6	Benedict, Uhlandstraße 49, 10719 Berlin
2	Wilmina (p. 53)	7	Dicke Wirtin, Carmerstraße 9, 10623 Berlin
3	Paris Bar (p. 115)	8	032c Store, Kantstraße 149, 10623 Berlin
4	Helmut Newton Foundation (p. 179)	9	C834 Corbusierhaus, Appartement 834 Ottmann
5	Galerie Friese (p. 173)		Flatowallee 16, 14055 Berlin

For years, all eyes were on the East. Mitte, Prenzlauer Berg, Friedrichshain, that was where the action was. But lately, Berliners have rediscovered the Old West. Charlottenburg and Wilmersdorf, once written off as bourgeois and a little too full of pensioners, suddenly feel relevant again.

The shift comes partly from housing pressures further east, but also from a new appreciation of West Berlin's elegance, the "old world". Broad boulevards, Art Nouveau facades, old cafés, and cultural landmarks now mix with a fresher wave of restaurants, boutique hotels, and design spaces. Charlottenburg, especially around Kantstraße and Savignyplatz, has found its rhythm—lively, international, and just the right amount of nostalgic.

Yes, some of the development feels slick and corporate (Bikini Berlin is more a lifestyle mall than an indie hub). But look closer and you'll find the area's real charm: literary cafés, smoky Wirtshäuser, experimental galleries, and landmarks of modernist architecture. West Berlin is no longer a relic, it's a city within the city, where old-world Paris vibes meet a distinctly Berlin edge.

Check in at one of Charlottenburg's cool hotels. The stylish Hoxton Charlottenburg or the poetic Wilmina, a boutique hotel in a former prison, are both excellent choices. Start the day at Benedict, where breakfast runs from early morning. To feel the aura of West Berlin glamour, stop by KaDeWe. The grand dame of Berlin shopping has been shining since 1907, with legendary food halls and a rooftop café. For culture, visit the Helmut Newton Foundation or make a pilgrimage to Le Corbusier's monumental Corbusierhaus. As evening falls, head back to Savignyplatz. Settle in for dinner at Dicke Wirtin or the iconic Paris Bar, where art still covers every wall. End the night on Kantstraße with cocktails at Green Door, hidden discreetly behind a buzzer.

Friedrichshain

			Don't miss:
1	Michelberger Hotel (p. 41)	4	Raw-Gelände, Revaler Str. 99, 10245 Berlin
2	Locke At Eastside Gallery (p. 45)	5	Shakespeare & Sons—Fine Bagels, Warschauer Str. 74, 10243 Berlin
3	Il Ritrovo (p. 111)	6	Küchenliebe, Gärtnerstraße 28, 10245 Berlin
		7	Flussbad Campus, Köpenicker Ch 3a, 10317 Berlin
		8	Eierhäuschen, Kiehnwerderallee, 12437 Berlin

"Friedrichshain is the neighbourhood that never delivered" was the word for many years. That was certainly the case when I first checked into the new Michelberger Hotel around 2009. Back then, Friedrichshain was raw and gritty, and stepping out of the Michelberger you'd close your eyes and head straight for Mitte.

Today, Friedrichshain delivers on all fronts. Sure, you'll still find anarchists with scruffy dogs but also young Gen-z families sunbathing on Boxhagener Platz. Graffiti continues to cover walls and façades, and on groundlevel the streets are buzzing with vegan restaurants, cafés, and independent shops. For the real, unfiltered Berlin experience, head to RAW-Gelände, where old industrial halls house a skatepark, techno clubs, beer gardens, and art.

Along Karl-Marx-Allee towards Mitte, you'll find monumental DDR-era architecture, in sharp contrast to the lively streets around Warschauer Straße and Oberbaumbrücke.

Revaler Straße and Simon-Dach-Straße have become one long party mile—the so-called "Techno Strich"—where twenty-something tourists spill into the streets on weekends. For many locals, it's a headache, bit the area is still in transition: a more grown-up crowd, better restaurants, and a new cosmopolitan energy is slowly taking over parts of Friedrichshain.

Allianz

5
6
3
9
11
4
10
8
7
12
1

Kreuzberg

1 Aerde (p. 87)
2 Annelies (p. 63)
3 Bonanza Coffee Roasters (p. 77)
4 Chungking Noodles (p. 81)
5 Gropius Bau (p. 177)
6 König Galerie (p. 183)
7 Helka Ceramics (p. 133)
8 Keit (p. 73)
9 ORA Restaurant & Wine (p. 107)
10 Original Unverpakt (p. 147)
11 Voo Store (p. 161)

Don't miss:
12 La Maison Berlin,
Paul-Lincke-Ufer 17
10999 Berlin

Kreuzberg is Berlin in its raw and mythical form. Once a refuge for squatters, punks, and political renegades, it has long been defined by a diverse mix of artists, radicals, bourgeois dreamers, and of course, the large Turkish community that has left an indelible mark on the neighbourhood.

Turkish markets overflow with spices and gözleme, while star chefs open restaurants in former corner pubs, emphasising the contrast between Kreuzberg's gritty, working-class past and its current wave of culinary gentrification and refinement.

The neighbourhood is broadly split in two: the western side, Kreuzberg 61 around Bergmannstraße and Chamissoplatz, and the eastern side, SO36 around Oranienstraße.

The 'polished' side is Kreuzberg 61, with its slightly bourgeois, provincial feel, and is home to some of Berlin's most important museums and galleries. Daniel Libeskind's dramatic Jewish Museum, Gropius Bau, and König Galerie, which is set inside a brutalist church, make this part of Kreuzberg a true art and culture destination. By contrast, SO36 around Oranienstraße, Kotti, remains the beating heart of Kreuzberg: chaotic, noisy, diverse, and full of energy. It's a mix of anti-establishment folk, great bars, and a large immigrant Turkish presence.

6
5
8
24
20
11
7
12
21
19
18
25
4
17
14
3
22
13
1
15
2
10
23
9
16

Mitte

1 Hotel Telegraphenamt (p. 17)
2 MM:NT (p. 21)
3 Father Carpenter (p. 91)
4 Clärchens Ballhaus (p. 85)
5 Frea Bakery (p. 71)
6 Coffee Circle Cafe (p. 65)
7 Zeit für Brot (p. 67)
8 Remi (p. 95)
9 Borchardt (p. 93)
10 Einstein (p. 75)
11 R.S.V.P Papier (p. 151)
12 Merz b. Schwanen (p. 139)
13 Adidas Originals (p. 125)
14 H&M Mitte Garten (p. 129)
15 Boros Sammlung (p. 167)
16 Holocaust Memorial (p. 191)
17 KW Institute for Contemporary Art (p. 181)
18 neugerriemschneider (p. 187)
19 Fotografiska Berlin (p. 171)
20 Do You Read Me?! (p. 155)

Don't Miss:

21 Strandbad Mitte, Kleine Hamburger Str. 16, 10117 Berlin
22 Lebensmittel in Mitte Rochstraße 2, 10178 Berlin
23 Freundschaft, Freundschaft
24 Pineapple Factory Gormannstraße 23, 10119 Berlin
25 Hamburger Bahnhof Invalidenstraße 50, 10557 Berlin

When you arrive in Berlin, Mitte is the natural first stop. The historic centre of the Old East. Here you'll find everything that makes the city famous, from culture, art, and shopping to restaurants and coffee bars. Mitte stretches across a wide area and is Berlin's central borough, but the part most closely associated with the neighbourhood feels far more intimate and easy to navigate, and it's exactly here that we begin.

Start at Hackescher Markt and follow the flow towards Rosenthaler Straße. Turn onto Alte or Neue Schönhauser Straße to explore design boutiques and high-street brands, or wander via Sophienstraße to Auguststraße and Linienstraße, where galleries like neugerriemschneider and cosy coffee or wine bars fill the old buildings.

Once the heart of East Berlin, with Alexanderplatz and the TV Tower as its backdrop, Mitte today is one of the city's most sought-after neighbourhoods. It's expensive, busy, and tourist-heavy, yes, but also home to some of Berlin's most stylish spots and a concentrated slice of urban life.

Stay at Hotel Telegraphenamt in the heart of Mitte. Start your morning at Zeit für Brot before heading to the Boros Collection for a guided tour through its striking bunker-turned-gallery. For lunch, stop by Lebensmittel in Mitte or the laid-back Strandbad Mitte, both local favourites. Spend the afternoon browsing nearby boutiques and design stores, then end the day at Clärchens Ballhaus to capture the charm of Berlin's golden dance-hall days.

LKW

TATRA
MOTOKOV

4
6
7
10
8
1
2
5
3
9

Neukölln

Don't miss:

1	JaJa (p. 103)	3	Imren Grill	7	Chrome Store
2	Neuzwei (p. 143)		Karl-Marx-Straße 75, 12043 Berlin		Lenaustraße 10, 12047 Berlin
		4	Osteria Sippi	8	Eins44
			Sanderstraße 10A, 12047 Berlin		Elbestraße 28/29, 12045 Berlin
		5	Paola Pinkel	9	Barra, Okerstraße 2, 12049 Berlin
			Karl-Marx-Straße 55, 12043 Berlin	10	Croissanterie
		6	The Good Store		Pannierstraße 56, 12047 Berlin
			Pannierstraße 31, 12047 Berlin		

Neukölln has gone from working-class grit to hipster darling in record time. Once the place artists and students moved to for cheap rents and shabby Altbau apartments, it's now a hub for creatives, freelancers, and young families. Turkish grocers and kebab shops still line the streets, but now they sit alongside galleries, natural wine bars, and vinyl cafés. The neighbourhood feels raw and global. English and Spanish are often heard more than German, thanks to the many creative newcomers.

Locals say the northern part of Neukölln within the S-Bahn ring already feels like Prenzlauer Berg did a decade ago, just with a more international edge. Around Weserstraße, the area has been ironically dubbed "Kreuzkölln," and is now becoming heavily touristed.

Heading out towards the "ring," you'll find things feel more authentic. Richardplatz, known to locals as Rixdorf, still retains its village-style architecture, although even here gentrification is increasingly putting pressure on the area. Start your day with coffee and a buttery croissant at Croissanterie, then grab one of Berlin's most famous kebabs for lunch at Imren Grill. Spend the afternoon treasure-hunting for vintage gems at Neuzwei at Neuzwei or the perfectly curated racks at The Good Store. As evening sets in, the neighbourhood's culinary side takes over. Go for Barra, where natural wines and Nordic minimalism meet Berlin charm, or dive into the colourful chaos of Paolo Pinkel, serving three cuisines under one roof. For something more refined, book a table at Eins 44, tucked inside a soaring old factory hall. After dark head back to Paolo Pinkel for its late-night buzz or settle into the natural wine bar at JaJa.

AYŞE
JUST
MISS PLATINUM IST TOLL
MARDY ARTS
frei
LH 600
VS 100
DER SACHE WEGEN
9051

26
HOTEL

7
6
10
1
2
9
5
4
8
3

Prenzlauer Berg

1 Gorki Apartments (p. 33)
2 The Circus Hotel (p. 37)
3 Acid Café (p. 59)
4 Chipperfield Kantine (p. 79)
5 Remi (p. 95)
6 Prater Biergarten (p. 121)
7 Frieda (p. 99)
8 The Store X Berlin (p. 157)

Don't Miss:
9 Supreme, Torstraße 74
10119 Berlin
10 L'Épicerie, Wörther Str. 19
10405 Berlin

Prenzlauer Berg has reinvented itself more than once. Once a run-down working-class district in old East Berlin, where buildings stood unrestored since the war, it later became a centre for punks and alternative culture. Today it's all latte art, organic supermarkets, yoga studios, and strollers lined up outside terrace cafés. Jugendstil facades and leafy boulevards frame a quarter filled with cafés, restaurants, and independent shops. Playgrounds and parks are everywhere, while Sundays in Mauerpark draw crowds for Berlin's most famous flea market and live music.

Sure, Prenzlauer Berg is gentrified and expensive, but also safe and undeniably beautiful. No wonder it's one of Berlin's most desirable family addresses. But Prenzlauer Berg isn't standing still; it's just moving in another direction. Where once prams filled every pavement, now you're just as likely to find fifty-something yuppie couples with teenage kids.

Start the day with coffee at Bonanza Coffee Roasters or opt for the laid-back vibe of Acid Café. For lunch head to David Chipperfield's own Kantine or to L'Épicerie, a tiny deli filled with French delights.

Prenzlauer Berg after dark used to be quiet, but things have changed, especially along Kastanienallee, which now buzzes with locals once night falls. Restaurants like Frieda and Remi serve up contemporary dining to a full crowd, or you can opt for traditional German food and a perfectly poured beer beneath the chestnut trees at Prater Biergarten, Berlin's oldest beer garden.

RGARTEN

1
7
3
2
5
6
8
9

Schöneberg-Tempelhof

			Don't Miss:
1	KaDeWe (p. 137)	5	Am Lok Depot, Am Lokdepot, 10965 Berlin
2	Aerde (p. 87)	6	Vej Coffee, Am Lokdepot 10, 10965 Berlin
3	Green Door (p. 117)	7	Jules cafe, Geisbergstraße 9, 10777 Berlin
4	Tempelhof Airport (p. 189)	8	Kunsthaus Dahlem, Käuzchensteig 12, 14195 Berlin
		9	Haus am Waldsee, Argentinische Allee 30, 14163 Berlin

Birthplace of Marlene Dietrich and home to David Bowie and Iggy Pop in the 1970s, Schöneberg carries a legendary cultural weight. And it was here in 1963, outside Rathaus Schöneberg, that John F. Kennedy declared, "Ich bin ein Berliner."

Another historical icon is the KaDeWe (Kaufhaus des Westens), Europe's most legendary department store. Opened in 1907, it became a symbol of West Berlin prosperity during the Cold War and remains a cathedral of consumption today.

Today, the district is Berlin's LGBTQ+ heartland, with rainbow flags waving from balconies, a thriving queer nightlife, and an easy-going lifestyle. Streets are lined with grand old buildings, playgrounds buzz with families, cafés spill onto pavements, and Berlin's largest weekly market unfolds across Winterfeldtplatz. Schöneberg has long been a stage for freedom and creativity, from 1920s cabarets to the LGBTQ+ movements of the 1980s, and the energy hasn't faded.

Architecture plays its part too. At Lokdepot, an experimental housing project rises from old railway grounds with recycled brick facades, greenhouse structures, and bold industrial detailing, a glimpse of Berlin's future living forms. Neighbouring Tempelhof is a study in reinvention: once an airport at the centre of world history, today a vast urban park. If you head further west, Kunsthaus Dahlem and Haus am Waldsee showcase Berlin's artistic and architectural heritage in two very different settings.

1
2
3
4
5
6
7

Tiergarten

			Don't Miss:
1	25hours Hotel Bikini Berlin (p. 25)	5	Andreas Murkudis, Potsdamer Str. 81, 10785 Berlin
2	SO/Berlin Das Stue (p. 29)	6	Oh, Panama, Potsdamer Str. 91, 10785 Berlin
3	Neue Nationalgalerie (p. 185)	7	Schleusenkrug, Müller-Breslau-Straße 14b
4	Bauhaus-Archiv (p. 193)		

Tiergarten is both park and political centre. A blend of nature, culture, and history. Here you'll find everything from Bauhaus classics to monuments, embassies, and art museums, all wrapped in green surroundings. Technically, Brandenburg Gate and the Holocaust Memorial belong to Mitte, but in real life, they're part of the Tiergarten route. Together with the Reichstag, they form a cluster of iconic landmarks that are usually visited at the same time.

South of Tiergarten, especially around Potsdamer Platz, you'll find embassies and government buildings. In the past, it was not a place anyone wanted to live. But the neighbourhood has changed significantly after the opening of Gleisdreieck Park and the luxury apartments towards Kreuzberg. Actually, the park is one of the best in the city, a lively green oasis where Berlin feels both urban and relaxed at the same time. In the corner sits BRLO Brwhouse, a microbrewery built from containers, where you can taste the house's own beers and modern street food in raw, industrial surroundings, making it a perfect stop after Tiergarten's more formal sights.

In the middle of Tiergarten park lies the city's green oasis with the Siegessäule as its golden centre. On warm days the paths fill with cyclists and picnics, while the beer garden spirit lives on at Schleusenkrug, a classic spot by the sluice on the Landwehrkanal. For a cultural pause, visit Mies van der Rohe's Neue Nationalgalerie nearby, a true modernist masterpiece.

Frieda

Lychener Strasse 37
10437 Berlin

@cafe_frieda
cafefrieda.de
+49 3044719800

On Helmholtzplatz in Prenzlauer Berg, Frieda reimagines the classic Berlin corner bistro with a modern, international twist. Drawing on both ancient and contemporary knowledge from European and Far Eastern traditions, they craft their own interpretation of the "modern urban kitchen." Opened in 2021 by Samina Raza and Ben Zviel, the duo behind Mrs. Robinson's, it has quickly become one of the city's most exciting dining rooms.

Here, the focus is on life's essentials: food, wine, vinyl, and good vibes. The menu shifts constantly with what's fresh at the markets, sourced from a network of small-scale farmers and fishers across Brandenburg and Europe. Expect oysters with tomato oil, lamb tartare with almonds, steak frites, or soft serve with seasonal toppings. Natural wines and vermouth dominate the drinks list, while the vinyl soundtrack adds to the laid-back, convivial atmosphere.

Frieda is the place for an unhurried dinner with friends, a spontaneous glass of pét-nat, or simply soaking up the neighbourhood's energy.

With Frieda, the founders reimagined the old Frida Kahlo on Helmholtzplatz as a café, bakery, wine bar, and dining room.

山下久美子
MODERNIST
BREAD
KYOTOFU

JaJa

Weichselstrasse 7
12043 Berlin

@jaja.berlin
jajawein.de
+49 30 52666911

Open since 2016 and run by French-German duo Julia Giese and Étienne Dodet, JaJa takes its name from a French slang word for everyday table wine, more rooted in French culture than German. Often cited as one of Europe's best natural wine bars, JaJa was also one of the first to push "natty" wine in Berlin, paving the way for places like Freundschaft and Barra.

Set on Neukölln's Weichselstraße, JaJa has become a city favourite. The list changes constantly, spanning reds, whites, and oranges from artisan producers across Europe, with a focus on low-intervention bottles from France and Spain. Minimal sulphites, maximum character. The idea from the beginning was to transplant Parisian natural wine culture into Berlin, not a bad idea.

But it's not just about the glass. JaJa frequently collaborates with chefs for pop-up dinners, while cheeses, charcuterie, fresh bread, and seasonal plates make easy companions to the wines. With exposed brick walls, chalkboard menus, and a lively street-side terrace, JaJa embodies the essence of Berlin's natural wine scene.

JaJa was one of the first to bring Parisian natural wine culture to Berlin, paving the way for a whole new wine scene.

RANIEN-APOTHEKE

ORA Restaurant & Wine Bar

Oranienplatz 14
10999 Berlin

@ ora.berlin
ora.berlin
+49 30 50955889

ORA is a wine bar and restaurant housed in the former Oranien pharmacy on Kreuzberg's Oranienplatz. In 2020, Nadine and Tom Michelberger, together with longtime Michelberger Hotel chef Alan Micks, took over the historic space and turned it into one of Berlin's most atmospheric dining rooms.

The cooking is seasonal and unfussy, with produce from small-scale farmers, foragers, hunters, and increasingly from the Michelberger farm in Spreewald. From early evening, the bar draws locals and visitors alike for oysters, small plates, and a constantly evolving wine list that swings from natural newcomers to classic estates.

With great attention to the historical details such as the elaborate woodwork and stucco from the 19th century, the former neighbourhood pharmacy was converted into a restaurant and bar in 2015 by its previous owners. The focus is on the original wooden fittings and the sales counter, which reflect the special charm of the place. Many historical objects such as crucibles and apothecary jars adorn the large wooden shelves and are reminiscent of the original use of the premises.

Step inside ORA and Kreuzberg's old apothecary soul still lingers in the woodwork and mirrors.

KEIN BOCK auf NAZIS
ZUM MITNEHMEN HIER BESTELLEN
GUEVARA

Il Ritrovo

Gabriel-Max-Strasse 2
10245 Berlin

ritrovo.de
+49 30 29364130

If you want slightly terrible service, wine served in cups, and seriously authentic Italian food, Il Ritrovo is your place. This Friedrichshain corner joint on Gabriel-Max-Straße has become a cult favourite where Berlin punk collides with rural Italian soul. The combination sounds crazy, but somehow it works.

The food is the star: oversized, wafer-thin pizzas with rustic toppings and bowls of pasta that are as generous as they are brilliant. Add brusque Italian waiters shouting across the room, scribbled walls, mismatched tables, and the result is chaotic charm at its finest. Families, students, and late-night locals all pile in, turning dinner into theatre.

Prepare to wait for a table during peak times, but come before 8pm on a Friday or Saturday, snag an outdoor seat, and you'll have front-row tickets to some of the best people-watching in Friedrichshain. It's cash only, no credit cards, no frills, just punk energy, pasta, pizza, and pure Berlin-Italian soul.

Freundschaft

Mittelstrasse 1
10117 Berlin

@bar_freundschaft

Located between Friedrichstraße station and the Humboldt University library, Freundschaft has been Berlin's most talked-about wine bar since Willi Schlögl and Johannes Schellhorn opened it in 2018. Tucked into the basement of the FAZ building, it sets the stage with a 26-metre-long oak bar, more a table than a counter, where wine is poured until late into the night.

The philosophy is simple: wine first, but never without camaraderie. The name Freundschaft means friendship, and the place lives up to it. The mood is sophisticated yet relaxed, designed for conversation and shared discovery rather than elitist performance. The wine list, 500+ bottles, is presented as a dark green tome, spanning Germany, Austria, France, Italy, Spain, and beyond, with a strong emphasis on natural and sustainable wines. Glass pours change daily, making each visit a fresh encounter.

Food plays a supporting but thoughtful role: compact plates of charcuterie, cheese, or Austrian-inspired comfort dishes that ensure, as the owners like to joke, "you don't get drunk too quickly."

ОТСТОИМ
ВОЛГУ-МАТУШКУ

Paris Bar

Kantstraße 152
10623 Berlin

@parisbar.berlin
parisbar.net
+49 3031380 52

Paris Bar is a relic and a theatre, a brasserie where Berlin's history is played out night after night. Opened in 1950 by a former French army cook, it became the city's bohemian living room in the Cold War years, when West Berlin was still an island adrift in the East. By the 1980s, it was the place to see and be seen: artists, actors, anarchists, and angels from Wim Wenders's Wings of Desire crowded into its red leather banquettes, whispering across starched tablecloths under the haze of cigarette smoke.

German playwrighter Heiner Müller called it "the hell of Berlin bars," a place where whiskey, cigars, and conversation stretched until dawn, when the paintings on the yellowed walls seemed to speak. Martin Kippenberger made it his home port, Fassbinder brought entire entourages, and Bowie and Iggy slipped in from their Schöneberg exile. Art and life blurred here, the walls layered with works gifted, loaned, or bartered, a salon hang that reads like a secret museum.

Today, Paris Bar still glows with that old West Berlin patina. Retro, eccentric, indispensable: a fossil perhaps, but one that still breathes. Step inside, and you enter a myth, a place where time folds, and the night never quite ends.

Green Door

Winterfeldtstrasse 50
10781 Berlin

@greendoorbar
www.greendoor.de
+49 302152515

Behind its emerald-painted door on Winterfeldstrasse hides one of Berlin's most legendary bars. Opened in 1995 by screenwriter and actor Fritz Müller-Scherz, Green Door was inspired by American jazz guitarist Eddie Condon and the secretive allure of Prohibition-era speakeasies, where a green door once signalled forbidden fun. Almost nothing has changed since: the blue-and-white checkered walls, the trowelled woodwork by artist Thomas Hauser, the well-worn chairs Fritz once shipped from New York.

After Fritz's death, his wife Andrea Kuhn, a dramaturg by trade, took over the business and determined to preserve the bar's soul while quietly modernising it. Under her care, and with bar manager Maria Gorbatschova at the helm, Green Door has become a benchmark for inventive mixology, earning multiple Mixology awards. The atmosphere remains intimate, layered with stories, from the python that once fell through the ceiling to the famous Rottweiler painting honouring Fritz's dog-loving mother.

Green Door, what's that secret you're keeping,
The Green Door, Jim Lowe 1956

EDDIE CONDON

PRATERGARTEN

Prater Biergarten

Kastanienallee 7–9
10435 Berlin

@pratergarten
pratergarten.de

On Kastanienallee in Prenzlauer Berg sits Berlin's oldest beer garden, a true institution dating back to 1837. For nearly two centuries, Prater Garten has welcomed locals to drink, eat, and watch theatre under its towering chestnut trees. Think of it, this place has survived two world wars, the GDR era, and reunification. In other words, there is history embedded in every corner here.

In summer, the Biergarten is the beating heart: long communal tables, dappled shade, and glasses of house-brewed Prater Pils or Schwarzbier, only available here. Add a Bratwurst or Obazda from the food stand and you have Berlin distilled into a single afternoon ritual. It's relaxed, convivial, and quintessentially local, where tourists, families, and hipsters all share benches.

But Prater Garten is not just for summer. The restaurant runs year-round, serving hearty German fare, schnitzel with Spargel in spring, roast goose in winter, in a setting that channels a 1920s Berlin vibe. Together, beer garden and restaurant make Prater not just a classic, but a living piece of Berlin.

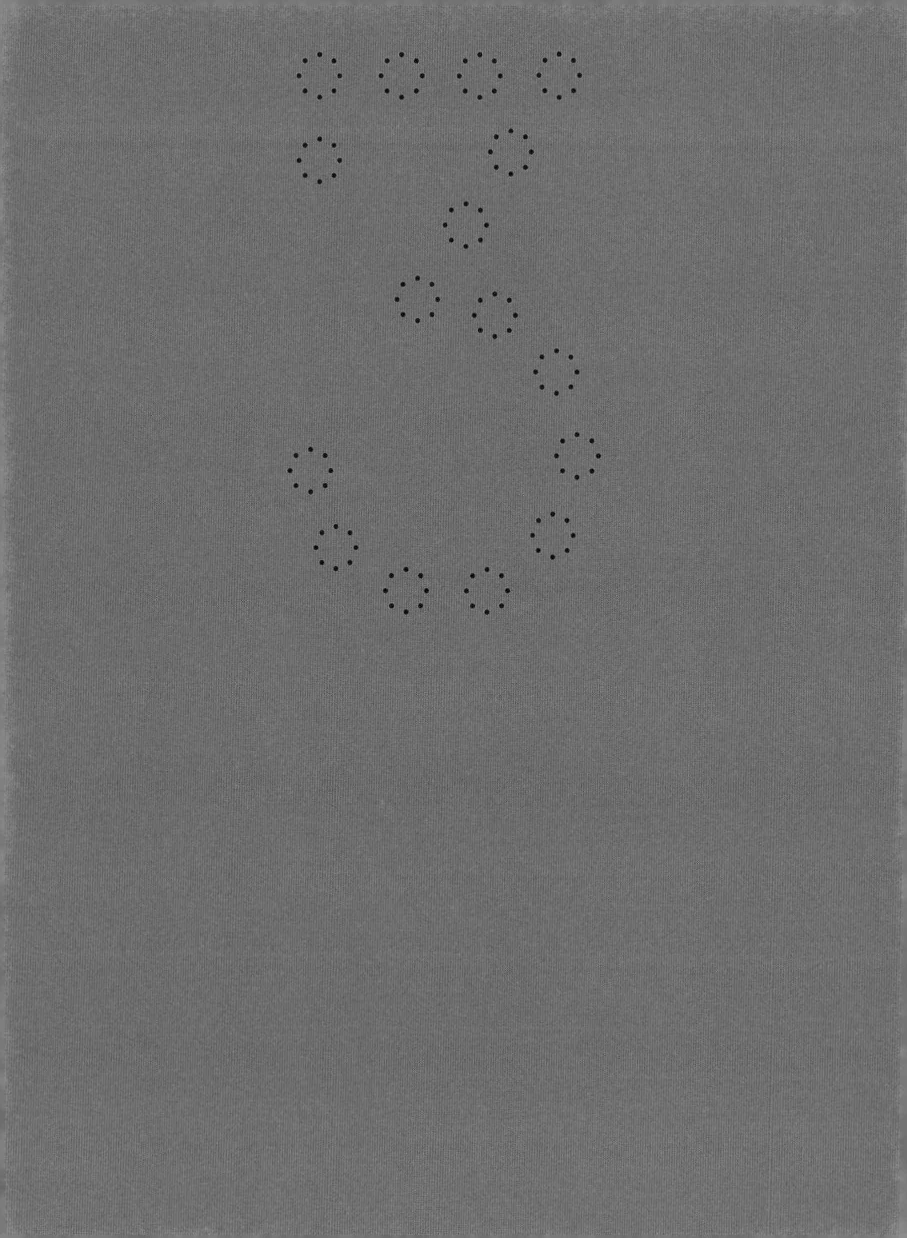

Adidas Originals Flagship Store

H&M Mitte Garten

Helka Ceramics

KaDeWe—Kaufhaus des Westens

Merz b. Schwanen

Neuzwei

Original Unverpakt

R.S.V.P Papier

Do You Read Me?!

The Store X Berlin

Voo Store

Shop

Adidas Originals Flagship Store

Münzstrasse 13–15
10178 Berlin

@adidasoriginals
adidas.com
+49 3072629798

Perhaps the best Adidas Originals Flagship Store, mixing lifestyle, fashion, and sport like no one else. Housed on Münzstraße between Hackescher Markt and Alexanderplatz, the Adidas Originals Flagship Store opened in 2014 as the brand's first flagship concept store in Germany. It quickly became one of the most important in Europe thanks to Berlin's unique streetwear and creative culture. Reimagined in 2020, it is now a dynamic space bringing shopping, street style, and creative culture together. The innovative store concept for Adidas Originals is called "The Collection", a mix of digital features, a sustainability hub, and a rotating edit of the most sought-after releases. Think of it less as retail, more as an experience.

Inside, stripped-back concrete and mod-industrial fixtures serve as the perfect backdrop for heritage sneakers and limited-edition drops. Walls are adorned with a 3D map of the neighbourhood and new interpretations of the iconic Trefoil logo, celebrating Berlin's Kiez culture and street heritage. The store is built around a feeling of community, more than just transactions: a space for people to interact with the brand, discover local artists displayed in the store, and explore new collaborations and products.

Recycling and sustainability are central elements in the interior concept. A bench salvaged from the 1972 Munich Olympics and flooring sourced from an old gym hall add layers of history, while a dedicated sustainability corner showcases Adidas' efforts to tackle plastic waste and rethink materials.

The Münzstraße flagship store laid the foundation, the first of its kind worldwide, and still the benchmark for adidas Originals.

// TEAKWONDO /// LOW PROFILE ///
A MELLOW CLASSIC
CAMPUS
3 STRIPES, CLASSIC SHELL TOE
SUPERSTAR
SUPERSTAR
3 STRIPES, CLASSIC SHELL TOE
SUPERSTAR

H&M
MITTE GARTEN
HENNES H&M MAURITZ
TTE GARTEN
HENNES H&M MAURITZ

H&M Mitte Garten

Neue Schönhauser Strasse 13
10178 Berlin

@hm
hm.com
+49 8006655900

I've been coming to this building for many years, and what makes it truly special is the mix of store, café, and the hidden backyard garden. A real urban oasis in Mitte.

H&M opened its concept and community store "Mitte Garten" here in September 2019, in the historic Volkscaféhaus on Neue Schönhauser Straße 13. Once home to the scene restaurant Schwarzenraben and later premium menswear store 14 oz., the listed 1891 building now houses H&M's first hyper-local flagship, developed by the brand's innovation lab.

It's one of the smallest and most curated H&M stores: a handpicked mix of collections, pre-loved fashion, collaborations, vintage pieces, and events, tailored for the local crowd. The design blends original details with greenery and light, extending into a 300 m^2 garden and a cosy café.

The combination of a truly unique H&M concept, a delicious vegetarian café, and the hidden garden out back makes this experience something special.

Cashmere

Helka Ceramics

Böckhstrasse 12
10967 Berlin

@helkagram
www.helkaceramics.com

Helka Ceramics is the kind of studio that makes you fall in love with clay all over again. Founded by Lisa Kosak in Berlin, the label is all about modern yet timeless tableware. Unique pieces that balance beauty and function so seamlessly they feel like old friends on your table. Everything is handmade in small batches on the potter's wheel in her Kreuzberg workshop, giving each cup, plate, or bowl its own quiet character. No two are alike, and that's exactly the point.

Beyond her collections, Lisa collaborates with restaurants, cafés, guesthouses, and hotels, creating bespoke ceramics that turn everyday rituals into small ceremonies. Helka Ceramics also hosts workshops and team-building sessions. After co-running another space for years, Lisa opened her own studio in Kreuzberg in 2023, a warm, creative hub where clay, community, and craftsmanship come together.

Hand-thrown in Kreuzberg, Helka Ceramics turns clay into quiet poetry.

RK-55

KAUFHAUS DES WESTENS
KaDeWe
THE
NEW
SEASON

KaDeWe– Kaufhaus des Westens

Tauentzienstrasse 21–24
10789 Berlin

@kadeweofficial
kadewe.de
+49 3021210

KaDeWe, or Kaufhaus des Westens, stands among the great European department stores, sharing its lineage with Galeries Lafayette in Paris, Selfridges in London, and La Rinascente in Milan, pioneers that revolutionised the very idea of shopping.

Since opening its doors in 1907, KaDeWe has survived two world wars, the division of Berlin, and reunification. Devastated during WWII, it was rebuilt to become a symbol of post-war recovery and, during the Cold War, a showcase of West Berlin's prosperity.

Rising over Tauentzienstraße like a temple to modern life, its eight floors cover 60,000 square metres, making it the largest department store on the European continent.

Today, Chanel and Dior sit alongside Berlin's own young labels; beauty halls gleam with Art Deco flair; and entire levels are devoted to home, living, and curated curiosities. But it is the sixth floor that defines KaDeWe's myth, the legendary food hall where locals, tourists and foodies lose themselves among oyster bars, truffle counters, and wine cellars, a global marketplace distilled into one address.

Merz b. Schwanen

Gormannstrasse 25
10119 Berlin

@merzbschwanen
merzbschwanen.com
+49 30 443189980

Merz b. Schwanen has become one of Berlin's most authentic fashion success stories. Known for loopwheeled tees and Henleys crafted with obsessive attention to detail, the brand has built a cult following among those who care about quality and timeless style.

Their flagship in Mitte, opened in 2022, reflects the same pared-back ethos: warm light, vintage German furniture, and rows of perfectly cut basics that feel anything but basic. Sustainability and slow fashion are central. Merz b. Schwanen speaks less about trends and more about timeless pieces.

The brand gained huge international exposure when Jeremy Allen White wore their classic white 215 tee in the hit series The Bear. Overnight, sales skyrocketed, launched the then-cult brand into the stratosphere.

Loopwheeled tees, crafted with devotion, now cult classics thanks to The Bear, this is the story of Merz b. Schwanen.

SEIT
1911
Merz b. Schwanen
BERLIN
STORE

Neuzwei

Weserstrasse 53
12045 Berlin

@neuzwei
neuzwei.com

Tucked away on Weserstraße in Neukölln, Neuzwei is one of those shops that feels more like a secret than a store. Founded in 2016 by Barbara Molnar, it quickly established itself as a go-to for timeless, high-quality pieces that outlast passing trends. The focus is on slow fashion and sustainable choices: think Levi's 501s, crisp silk blouses, and carefully curated accessories that feel both classic and current.

Alongside vintage finds, you'll spot labels like Laura Lombardi and The Nude Label, all selected with Barbara's sharp eye for design, natural fabrics, and enduring style. Every garment is in impeccable condition, making browsing here less about rummaging and more about discovering.

The interior, furnished with self-designed wooden pieces, adds to the calm and understated charm of the shop. And it's Barbara's own warmth and sensitivity that make the atmosphere feel so inviting.

Looking for that specific Y2K piece from Gucci?
There is a pretty good chance you'll find it at Neuzwei.

Gutes

Original Unverpakt

Wiener Strasse 16
10999 Berlin

@originalunverpackt
original-unverpackt.de

When Original Unverpackt opened a shop in Kreuzberg it sparked a movement. As Germany's first supermarket to ditch single-use packaging entirely, it rewrote the rules of how we shop. Forget endless plastic wrappers: here you bring your own jars, bottles, and bags, or borrow reusable containers in-store, and fill them with exactly what you need. No more, no less.

The shelves are lined with organic pantry staples, spices, and snacks, alongside eco-friendly cleaning products, soaps, and clever low-waste alternatives for everyday life. But the real innovation isn't the goods themselves, it's the mindset. Original Unverpackt makes sustainable consumption feel easy, stylish, and strangely liberating.

More than a store, it's a manifesto in action: proof that shopping can be conscious, transparent, and future-minded without losing the joy of discovery.

Original Unverpackt represents a quiet retail revolution that began right here in Berlin.

OU
OU
1,50 €
OU
0,39 €
OU
0,39 €

F O O D
EAST END PRESS

R.S.V.P Papier

Mulackstrasse 26
10119 Berlin

@rsvpberlin
rsvp-berlin.de
+49 3031956410

Hidden in the heart of Mitte, R.S.V.P. Papier has been Berlin's go-to for stationery lovers since 2001, like a cabinet of curiosities for paper and pen enthusiasts. Think Japanese notebooks, Swiss precision pencils, and timeless brands like Caran d'Ache, OHTO, Koh-I-Noor, and Kaweco, all arranged with the kind of care usually reserved for galleries.

R.S.V.P. celebrates the slow beauty of craft. Classic techniques like letterpress, silkscreen, risography, and steel engraving are kept alive here, producing limited-edition cards and paper goods in collaboration with artists and designers from around the world, from Japan to Portugal, from Korea to the US. Alongside, you'll find calendars, wall planners, and tools you didn't know you needed: staple-free staplers, elegant steel rulers, folding bones.

At R.S.V.P. Papier, every visit brings new surprises, and even the gift wrapping is part of the experience.

Aster
Handkoloriert
Made in the U.K.
7,90 Euro

Parks
TO
THINK
ORDINARY
YOLO
032c
AFGHANS
PIN-UP
11 Film
irin
Riposte
愉悦
Bastard Cookbook
Antto Melasniemi
Rirkrit Tiravanija

Do You Read Me?!

Auguststrasse 28
10117 Berlin

@doyoureadme_berlin
doyoureadme.de
+49 3069549695

Do You Read Me?! is an internationally recognised presence in the world of printed matter. Founded by Mark Kiessling in 2008, the tiny but mighty independent bookstore is known for its inspiring curation and expert perspective on contemporary print and publishing. From its buzzing storefront in Berlin to global collaborations in Basel, Copenhagen, Helsinki, Tokyo, Sydney and New York, do you read me?! has established itself not only as a place to simply buy (fantastic) books and magazines, but as a dynamic cultural space fostering conversations across disciplines, from art and architecture to photography, design, theory, food, and fashion.

The Store X Berlin

Torstrasse 1
10119 Berlin

@thestoresx
thestorex.com
+49 30 405044550

Launched in 2015 and curated by British fashion director Alex Eagle, The Store X was born from Soho House's vision to blur the boundaries between retail, hospitality, and culture. The concept is simple but radical: a space where you can shop, eat, work, and hang out, and where everything, from the candle burning on the table to the sofa beneath you, is for sale.

Housed within Soho House Berlin in Mitte, the two-storey space feels like a cross between gallery and living room. Industrial concrete pillars are softened by mid-century furniture, curated bookshelves, and rotating art installations, creating an atmosphere that is both raw and refined.

Fashion takes centre stage with a sharp edit that has included Balenciaga, Jil Sander, The Row, Issey Miyake, and Proenza Schouler, while shelves extend into design objects, music, and beauty.

One of Berlin's most forward-thinking cultural destinations, part retail, part hangout, fully immersive.

NIKE
NIKE
NIKE

Voo Store

Oranienstrasse 24
10999 Berlin

@voostore
voostore.com
+49 3061651112

Berlin's most influential concept spaces and a must-see destination. Tucked inside a 300-square-metre courtyard on Oranienstraße in Kreuzberg, the store reflects the neighbourhood's eclectic energy and the city's creative spirit.

Founded by brothers Kaan and Yasin Müjdeci, one a film director, the other an entrepreneur, Voo Store has always been more than just retail. It's a concept store where fashion, design, art, and community intersect.

The selection is broad yet carefully curated: from high fashion to streetwear, from design objects and books to sneakers and jewellery. Expect Prada next to Acne Studios, Nike alongside experimental labels and emerging talent. The guiding principle is simple: pieces should outlast trends and carry value beyond a single season.

Inside, raw walls and exposed brick from its workshop past set an atmosphere of authenticity and understated elegance. Voo Deli adds another layer, serving natural wines, organic food, and carefully selected deli essentials, alongside coffee and pastries with seating spilling into the leafy courtyard.

Simply Berlin's most influential concept store and a destination not to be missed.

VOO

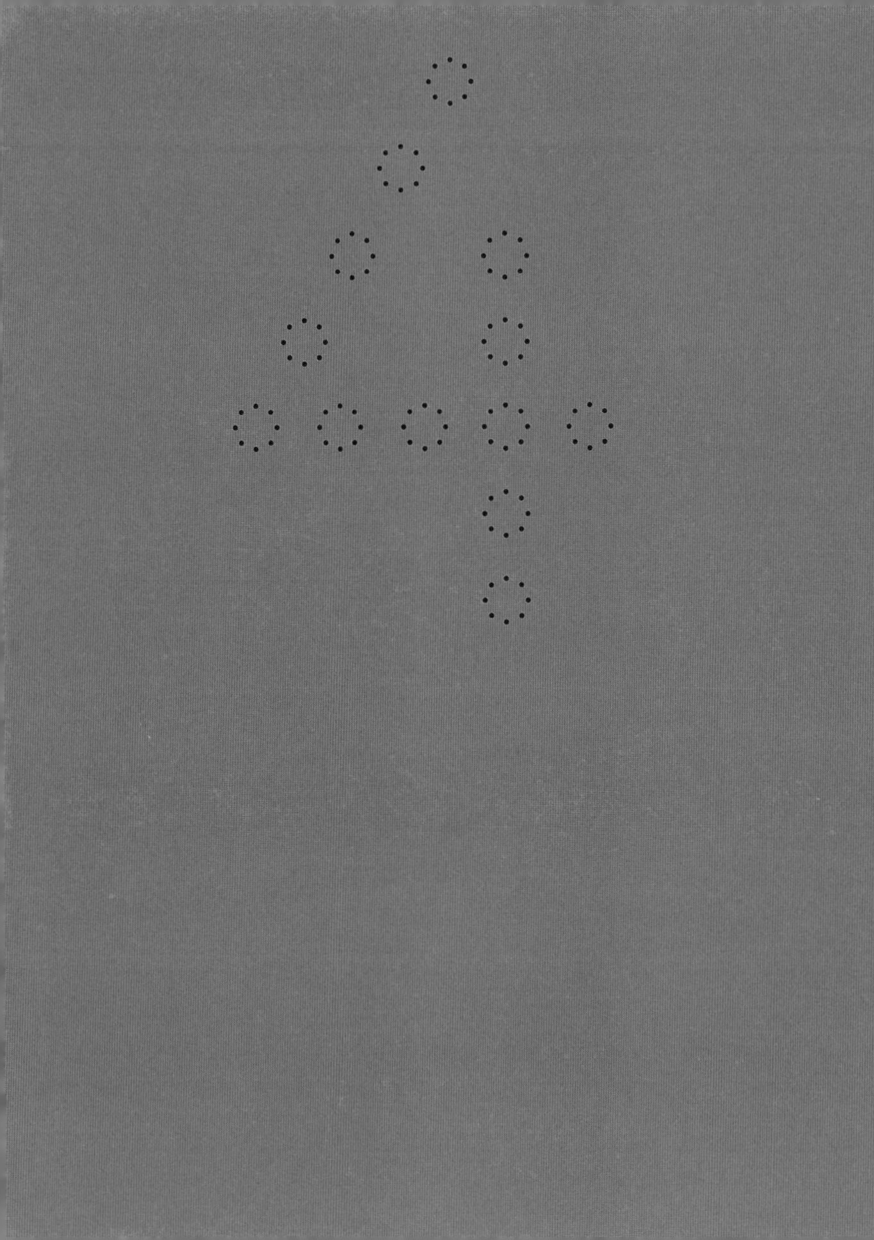

Boros Sammlung
Fotografiska Berlin
Galerie Friese
Gropius Bau
Helmut Newton Foundation
Kw Institute for Contemporary Art
KÖNIG GALERIE
Neue Nationalgalerie
neugerriemschneider
Tempelhof
The Holocaust Memorial
Bauhaus-Archiv

Explore

Boros Sammlung

Reinhardtstrasse 20
10117 Berlin

@boroscollection
sammlung-boros.de/
+49 3027594065

Few art collections in Berlin come with a backdrop as charged as the Boros Sammlung. Housed in a concrete bunker near Friedrichstrasse, the space carries the scars and stories of 20th-century Germany. Built in 1942 as an air-raid shelter, it went on to serve many lives: a Red Army prison, a textile warehouse, and, in the GDR years, the city's so-called "banana bunker" storing tropical fruit. After reunification, it became notorious in the 1990s as a techno temple and site for experimental theatre, fetish parties, even a short-lived sex fair.

In 2003, Christian and Karen Boros bought the building and transformed it into a private museum for their contemporary art collection. The conversion, completed in 2007, carved intimate white cubes and dramatic concrete voids into the wartime shell, creating a visceral setting where art and history collide. Since opening in 2008, the Boros Collection has been presented in rotating chapters, each featuring a new constellation of international artists—from Olafur Eliasson, Ai Weiwei, and Wolfgang Tillmans to Anne Imhof, Alicja Kwade, and Julius von Bismarck.

A private art collection hidden in an old WW2 bunker.

EXHIBITIONS

Fotografiska Berlin

Oranienburger Str. 54
10117 Berlin

@fotografiska.berlin
berlin.fotografiska.com

Housed in a historic building shaped by Berlin's layered past, Fotografiska Berlin redefines what a museum for contemporary photography can be, feeling less like a traditional institution and more like a dynamic cultural hub. Founded in Stockholm in 2010, Fotografiska has grown into a global institution, yet each location carries its own distinct identity, and Berlin, which opened in 2023 in the former The Kunsthaus Tacheles building, is no exception.

Across several floors, a constantly evolving exhibition programme brings together internationally acclaimed photographers and emerging local talents. The curation leans towards the thought-provoking rather than the predictable, inviting visitors to engage with visual storytelling that challenges perspectives and reflects the world we live in.

But Fotografiska is more than exhibitions. It's a place where photography meets conversation, dining, and late-night culture, creating an experience that extends well beyond the gallery walls.

With sister museums in cities like New York, Tallinn, Oslo and Shanghai, Fotografiska's mission remains clear: to inspire a more conscious world through the power of photography.

Galerie Friese

Meierottostrasse 1
10719 Berlin

@galeriefriese
galeriefriese.de
+49 3088711371

Overlooking Fasanenplatz in Berlin's former gallery district, Galerie Friese bridges past and present with ease. Founded in Stuttgart in 2008 and relocated to Charlottenburg in 2015, it has become a key address for cultural exchange in the city.

The gallery's focus lies in painting and drawing, but always across epochs. Classical modernism meets contemporary practice, allowing themes, techniques, and ideas to echo across generations. This cross-epochal approach keeps the programme fresh, highlighting how historic movements resonate with today's artistic voices.

Talks, publications, and curated events turn Galerie Friese into a space for dialogue, where context matters as much as the work on the walls. It's this blend of scholarship, mediation, and curatorial experimentation that makes Friese stand out.

In a neighbourhood long associated with avant-garde pioneers, Galerie Friese continues the tradition: a place where history informs the present, and the future of art feels within reach.

Galerie Friese turns art history into an ongoing conversation in the heart of Charlottenburg.

Gropius Bau

Niederkirchnerstrasse 7
10963 Berlin

@gropiusbau
berlinerfestspiele.de/gropius-bau
+49 30254860

The Gropius Bau is one of Berlin's most important cultural addresses. An institution where art doesn't just hang on walls but spills into conversations, performances, and experiments. Located in a beautiful grand 19th-century building designed by Martin Gropius and Heino Schmieden, it was once a museum and school of decorative arts. Today, it's a space for contemporary artists, who often take up residencies in its studios, shaping the programme from the inside out. Exhibitions range from global heavyweights to immersive thematic shows, all bound by a spirit of exchange and openness.

Part of the Berliner Festspiele since 2001, the Gropius Bau is as much about ideas as objects. The building itself tells a story of resilience, badly bombed in WWII, nearly demolished, then rescued in the 1960s by Walter Gropius, the Bauhaus founder and nephew of Martin Gropius. Reconstruction preserved mosaics and reliefs alongside deliberate scars of destruction, a reminder that culture in Berlin is always layered: history and reinvention, loss and creation, side by side.

Helmut Newton Foundation

Jebensstrasse 2
10623 Berlin

@helmutnewtonfoundation
helmutnewton.com
+49 3031864825

The Helmut Newton Foundation is Berlin's temple to one of fashion photography's most provocative and stylish figures. Founded by Newton himself in 2003, just months before his death, it was never meant to be a mausoleum but a living stage for dialogue. Alongside Newton's daring, cinematic images, often celebrated and scandalous in equal measure, the shows are curated in conversation with other heavyweights: Mario Testino, Sarah Moon, David LaChapelle, Paolo Roversi, and even David Lynch have all been hung here.

The permanent exhibition, Private Property, reveals a more intimate side, displaying Newton's cameras, personal effects, and work tools, while the rotating shows keep his legacy in motion, never frozen. Set within the former Landwehrkasino near Zoologischer Garten, the space itself adds grandeur to the mix, a fitting backdrop for photography that blurred lines between art, fashion, and provocation.

Today the Foundation is not just a Berlin must-see but an international hub, touring Newton's vision worldwide while continuing to ask: what is beauty, and who gets to frame it?

KW

KW Institute for Contemporary Art

Auguststrasse 69
10117 Berlin

@kwinstitutefcontemporaryart
kw-berlin.de
+49 30 24345969

KW Institute for Contemporary Art, or simply KW, is one of the pillars of Berlin's contemporary art scene. Founded in the early 1990s by Klaus Biesenbach and collaborators in a disused margarine factory in Mitte, it quickly became a catalyst for Berlin's rise as an international art capital.

What sets KW apart is its restless energy. With no permanent collection, it operates more like a kunsthalle, a flexible exhibition space dedicated to temporary shows, commissions, and collaborations.

Through exhibitions, performances, talks, and commissioned works, KW has consistently placed itself at the centre of both local and global cultural discourse.

Over three decades on, KW remains as vital as ever: a dynamic hub where progressive practices meet bold curatorial ideas, and where Berlin's raw, experimental spirit still finds a home.

KÖNIG GALERIE

Alexandrinenstrasse 118–121
10969 Berlin

@koeniggalerie
koeniggalerie.com
+49 30 26103080

KÖNIG GALERIE has become one of Berlin's most influential platforms for contemporary art. Founded by Johann König in 2002, the gallery quickly built a reputation for championing both emerging and established voices, often with a focus on younger generations. Its programme spans the full spectrum of media, sculpture, painting, video, installation, photography, and performance, always with a concept-driven edge.

Since 2015, its flagship has been St. Agnes, a monumental Brutalist church in Kreuzberg designed by Werner Düttmann in the 1960s. Respectfully reimagined by architect Arno Brandlhuber, the building is now an icon of Berlin's cultural landscape and was awarded the Berlin Architecture Prize in 2016.

But König's ambitions stretch well beyond Berlin. In recent years the gallery has expanded with pop-ups in London, Tokyo, Vienna, Monaco, and Munich, while opening permanent branches in Seoul (2021) and Mexico City (2024). Back home, a second Berlin space opened in 2025 at the historic Telegraphenamt, further cementing König's presence in the city.

Today, works from KÖNIG artists are represented in major institutions worldwide, including MoMA and the Guggenheim, while its artists continue to headline biennials and landmark exhibitions. More than a gallery, KÖNIG is a global stage shaped in Berlin.

Neue Nationalgalerie

Potsdamer Strasse 50
10785 Berlin

@neuenationalgalerie
smb.museum
+49 30266424242

Mies van der Rohe's final masterpiece, the Neue Nationalgalerie, landed in 1968 like a UFO of modernism. A vast steel roof hovers over glass walls, the whole thing stripped of columns to create one radical open space. Minimal, monumental, and impossibly cool, it's both a shrine to modernism and Mies's last word on architecture.

Built as part of Hans Scharoun's Kulturforum, the museum sat on the edge of West Berlin, a cultural counterweight to Museum Island in the East. Its opening felt like a statement: continuity and new beginnings, all under one floating roof. Inside, the "Gallery of the 20th Century" gave a divided city a way to reclaim its modern heritage. After five decades of heavy use, the building was restored between 2015 and 2021, polishing up the glass and steel while keeping Mies's vision intact.

Today, the Neue Nationalgalerie presents rotating exhibitions from the Nationalgalerie's 20th-century collection. To enter its glass walls is to experience art and architecture in dialogue, Berlin's modernist crown jewel, still as radical and relevant today as it was in 1968.

neugerriemschneider

Linienstrasse 155
10115 Berlin

neugerriemschneider.com
+49 3028877277

Founded in 1994 by Tim Neuger and Burkhard Riemschneider, neugerriemschneider has long been one of the key destinations in Berlin's art world. A first-mover from the start, giving early solo shows to then-unknowns like Olafur Eliasson and Michel Majerus, both of whom went on to become defining figures of their generation. Over the years, the gallery has steadily expanded its reach, building a roster that today includes international heavyweights such as Ai Weiwei and Thomas Bayrle, while continuing to nurture new voices.

The gallery's programme has always been less about chasing trends and more about shaping them. Shows often lean toward installation and conceptual art, yet the real signature is how artists are given space to test ideas and experiment, something that has made neugerriemschneider a touchstone for institutions and collectors alike.

With two locations in Berlin, the gallery is deeply woven into the city's cultural fabric, while its presence at leading art fairs keeps it firmly on the international stage. neugerriemschneider is not just a gallery to visit, but a place to understand how Berlin became, and remains, one of the world's contemporary art capitals.

Tempelhof

Platz d. Luftbrücke 5
12101 Berlin

@flughafentempelhof_thf
thf-berlin.de
+49 30 2000374261

Few places in Berlin embody history and reinvention quite like Tempelhof. Opened in 1923, the airport became one of the world's largest buildings and a symbol of modern aviation. It was here that the Berlin Airlift of 1948–49 unfolded, when American and British planes landed every few minutes, with food and supplies for a city under blockade. Those vast runways, once the stage for Cold War survival, are now where Berliners jog, cycle, or fly kites in the summer wind.

For decades it functioned as West Berlin's international gateway, a showcase of resilience in the shadow of the Wall. Closed in 2008, its monumental scale remains unmatched, an architectural relic whose concrete mass and sweeping hangars still radiate the weight of history, even as Berliners picnic, cycle, and relax in Tempelhofer Feld.

The Holocaust Memorial

Cora-Berliner-Strasse 1
10117 Berlin

stiftung-denkmal.de
+49 302639430

The Memorial to the Murdered Jews of Europe is one of Berlin's most powerful and unsettling landmarks. Opened in 2005, it consists of 2,711 concrete stelae designed by architect Peter Eisenman, spread across a sloping field in the heart of the city. Walking through the grid, the blocks rise and fall around you, creating a shifting landscape that feels at once ordered and disorienting, a physical metaphor for loss, memory, and the impossibility of comprehension.

The idea for the memorial began in the late 1980s, driven by journalist Lea Rosh and historian Eberhard Jäckel, and was officially approved by the Bundestag in 1999. Beneath the site lies the Information Centre, documenting the names, stories, and histories of Holocaust victims. Together, the memorial and its underground archive form a place of reflection that is less about closure and more about confronting absence, an essential stop for anyone seeking to understand Berlin's layered history.

Bauhaus-Archiv

Knesebeckstrasse 1
10623 Berlin-Charlottenburg

@bauhaus_archiv
bauhaus.de
+49 302 540 020

The Bauhaus-Archiv / Museum für Gestaltung owns the world's largest collection of Bauhaus works and is an international research centre dedicated to studying the history and influence of this famous school of art and design (1919–1933). The museum, which was designed by Bauhaus founder Walter Gropius, opened its doors in 1979. Since 2018, the historic building has undergone extensive renovation in accordance with landmark preservation guidelines. A new museum annex, designed by the Berlin-based architecture firm Staab Architekten, will provide a generous addition to its exhibition space and includes a visually striking glass tower, which will be primarily used for educational purposes.

Until the reopening, the Temporary Bauhaus-Archiv in Berlin-Charlottenburg is hosting a varied programme. It deals with the Bauhaus-Archiv's collection as well as current topics relating to design, architecture, and society. On Saturdays, the "Bauhaus Lab" invites interested people of all ages to get creative together. The Temporary Bauhaus-Archiv also houses the Bauhaus-Shop with objects for everyday use, from original Bauhaus designs to contemporary design.

Index

13
TIERGARTEN
CHARLOTTENBURG-WILMERSDORF
4
49
56
52
10
3
31
37
9
47
32
22

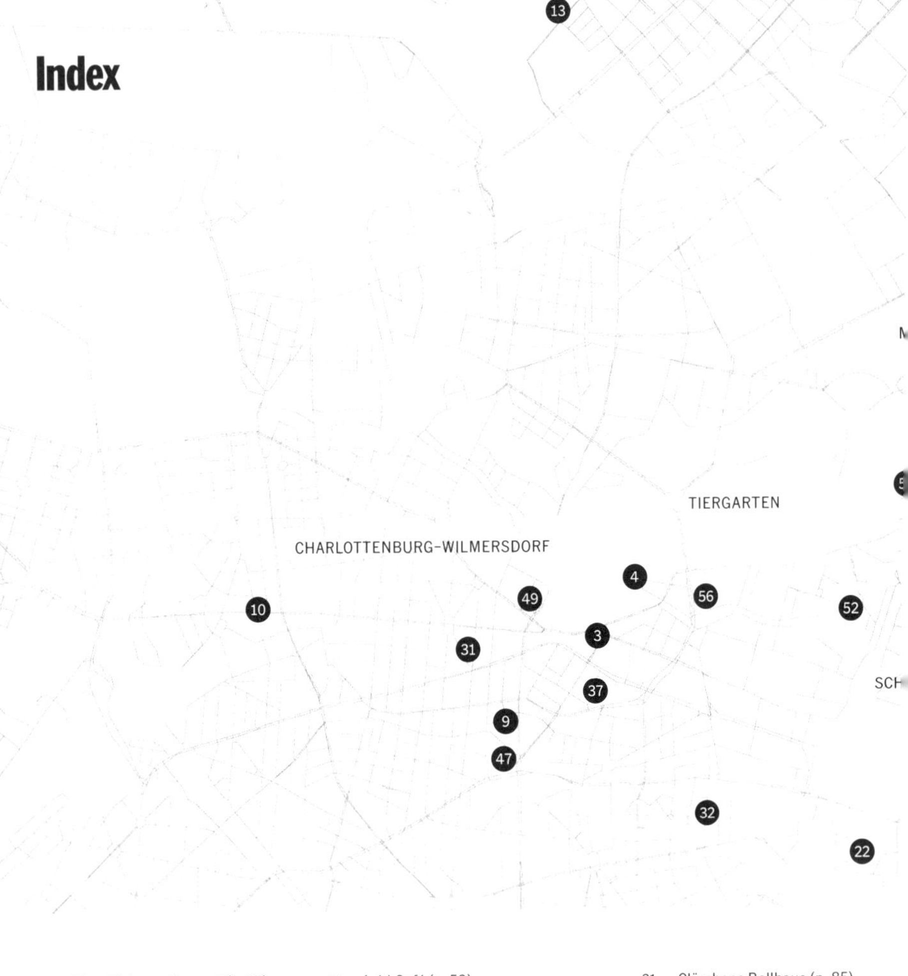

Scan to get the map

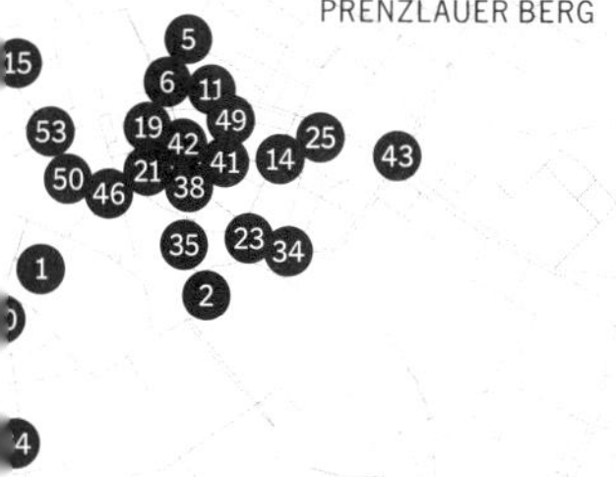

CHSHAIN
ZBERG

NEUKÖLLN

LHOF

Mads Arlien-Søborg is a Copenhagen-based journalist and lifestyle expert. He holds a master's degree in modern Culture and Communication from University of Copenhagen. Mads has worked with design, fashion and lifestyles for many years. He has hosted several television shows about travel, design and architecture.

New Mags is more than a bookstore; it's a destination where art and literature converge, offering a select array of lifestyle books, magazines, and accessories. Founded in 2016 in Horsens, Jutland by Jesper Svangård and Jesper Oxholm Mikkelsen. Their dream of a space that not only stores but celebrates books culminated in the opening of their first showroom in Copenhagen in 2021.

NOTES

NOTES

NOTES

Front cover:
© Mads Arlien-Søborg

Destination:
© Pexels / Sally Rango / Mads Arlien-Søborg

Neighbourhoods:
© Unsplash / Mads Arlien-Søborg / KLU-Berlijn / Carolin Weinkopf / Pexels / Sally Rango / Claudius Pflug_Tempelhof Projekt GmbH

Stay:
Hotel Telegraphenamt: © Tobias Koppisch
MM:NT: © Silke Briel
25hours Hotel Bikini Berlin: © Stephan Lemke
Das Stue: Courtesy of Das Stue
Gorki Apartments: Courtesy of Gorki Apartments
The Circus Hotel: © Carolin Weinkopf
Michelberger Hotel: © Philipp Obkircher / Sigurd Larsen Design & Architecture
Locke at East Side Gallery: © Nicholas Worley
The Hoxton Charlottenburg: Courtesy of The Hoxton
Wilmina: © Wilmina | Photo: Markus Gröteke / Bocci, photo: Harry Fricker / Wilmina, photo: Patricia Parinejad

Taste:
Paris Bar: © Ernst Arno Baur
Aerde Restaurant: © Oliver Helbig and Raaago
Bonanza Coffee Roasters: © Modiste Studio
Chungking Noodles: © Fanette Guilloud
Annelies: © Noel Richter
Il Ritrovo: © Mads Arlien-Søborg
Chipperfield Kantine: © Marion Schoenenberger / Courtesy of Ute Zscharnt
Remi: © Robert Rieger
Father Carpenter: © Mads Arlien-Søborg
Clärchens Ballhaus: © Jonas Kolahdoozan / Courtesy of Clärchens Ballroom
Frea Bakery: © Cristobal / 8.a.m
Coffee Circle Café: Courtesy of Coffee Circle Café
Zeit für Brot: Courtesy of Zeit für Brot
Prater Biergarten: © Mads Arlien-Søborg
Frieda: Courtesy of Frieda
Borchardt: Courtesy of Borchardt
Einstein: Courtesy of Einstein
Acid Café: © Daniel Farò
Keit: © Michael-Burman
JaJa: © gushy.me
Freundschaft: © Ingo Pertramer
ORA Restaurant & Wine Bar: © Zoe Spawton, Diana Nagirnyak
Green Door: © Katja Hiendlmayer

Shop:
R.S.V.P Papier in Mitte: © Martin Pauer
Merz b. Schwanen Store: © Peter Plotnicki
Voo Store: © Voo Store
Helka Ceramics: © Daniel Farò
Original Unverpackt © JuanaK Klein, Fotobäckerei, Pauline Kluschke, Ben Mönks
The Store X Berlin: Courtesy of The Store X Berlin
Neuzwei: Courtesy of Neuzwei
Originals Flagship Store Berlin: © Oliver Müller Fotografie, www.olivermlr.com
H&M Mitte Garten: Courtesy of H&M
Do You Read Me?!: © Schmott Studios

Explore:
Martin-Gropius-Bau: © Gropius Bau, photo: Robert Rieger and Frank Sperling
König Galerie: © Roman März / Courtesy of König Galerie
Bauhaus-Archiv: © visitberlin, photo: Wolfgang Scholvien
Boros Collection: © Noshe
Hamburger Bahnhof: © Staatliche Museen zu Berlin, photo: David von Becker
Holocaust Memoria: © Foundation Memorial, photo: Marko Priske
KW Institute for Contemporary Art: © David von Becker
Helmut Newton Foundation: © Stefan Müller
Haus am Waldsee: © Deborah Mittelstaedt
Galerie Friese: © Eric Tschernow.
Neue Nationalgalerie: © Staatliche Museen zu Berlin, photo: David von Becker
neugerriemschneider: © Pawel Althamer
Fotografiska Berlin: © Pion Studio
Bauhaus Archiv: © Marcus Ebener

NEW MAGS CITY GUIDE
BERLIN

Editor-In-Chief: Mads Arlien-Søborg
Publisher: New Mags
Sales: Jesper Svangård, New Mags

Art Direction: Studio8585
Design Director: Mario Depicolzuane
Design & Layout: Benja Pavlin, Varshini KVSS

ISBN: 97887-85374-22-6

1st Edition 2026
Printed at Print Best, Estonia, 2026

Published in 2026 by New Mags
& Helmin Publishing

New Mags, Office & Distribution
Vejlevej 13, 8700 Horsens, Denmark
new-mags.com

NEW MAGS

Helmin Publishing
Nivå Strandpark 21, 1, 2990 Nivå, Denmark
helminpublishing.dk

This book contains a curated selection of the editor's favourite places and should be used for its intended purpose, as a guide. It is by no means comprehensive of all the amazing locations the city has to offer. Since changes may have occurred since publication, we recommend using the contact information for each location to ensure up-to-date details.

The editor and publisher wish to express their gratitude to everyone who played a role in making this book possible: the staff, friends and families, brands, and organizations. A big thank you to Fujifilm® for giving us the opportunity to create beautiful city images for the book.